A Year of Vincentian Preaching
by Daniel Harris, CM

A Year of Vincentian Preaching by Daniel Harris, CM

Gregory Heille, OP,
AND
Emmanuel Diaz,
EDITORS

RESOURCE *Publications* • Eugene, Oregon

A YEAR OF VINCENTIAN PREACHING BY DANIEL HARRIS, CM

Copyright © 2022 Gregory Heille, OP, and Emmanuel Diaz. All rights reserved. Except for brief quotations in critical publications or reviews, no part of this book may be reproduced in any manner without prior written permission from the publisher. Write: Permissions, Wipf and Stock Publishers, 199 W. 8th Ave., Suite 3, Eugene, OR 97401.

Resource Publications
An Imprint of Wipf and Stock Publishers
199 W. 8th Ave., Suite 3
Eugene, OR 97401

www.wipfandstock.com

PAPERBACK ISBN: 978-1-6667-5376-9
HARDCOVER ISBN: 978-1-6667-5377-6
EBOOK ISBN: 978-1-6667-5378-3

10/11/22

Contents

Remembering Dan Harris | vii
—Gregory Heille, OP

Daniel Harris, Vincentian | xi
—Anthony J. Dosen, CM

Daniel Harris, Parish Preacher | xv
—James Cormack, CM

Daniel Harris, Seminary Preaching Teacher | xix
—Gregory Heille, OP

Preaching Through the Liturgical Year by Daniel Harris, CM
—Edited by Emmanuel Diaz

Advent | 3
Christmas | 16
Lent | 33
Easter | 51
Sunday Feasts in Ordinary Time | 75
Bread of Life Discourse | 92
Mary, the Angels, and St. Vincent de Paul | 108

Remembering Dan Harris

Gregory Heille, OP

One of my favorite memories of Dan Harris is how his whole face would light up whenever he walked into the school's coffee room at the beginning of the day and discovered "Donuts!" No doubt, Dan would laugh to hear me say that, but whenever I mention his name, people's faces still light up to remember his gift of joy and quirky sense of humor.

For the forty-two years of his Vincentian priesthood, Dan worked Monday to Friday as a seminary teacher of preaching and then preached for religious sisters and at parishes on Saturday and Sunday. Dan's *joie de vivre* expressed Christian faith in what Pope Francis calls the joy of the gospel. If Pope Francis had heard Dan, I am sure he would have heard the gospel joy overflowing in Dan's preaching.

From Dan's priestly ordination in 1974 to his death in 2016, that same gospel joy found expression as he taught preaching at several seminaries. Dan's teaching included sixteen years in two terms at Kenrick-Glennon Seminary in St. Louis, two years at DeAndreis Institute of Theology in Lemont, Illinois, two years at St. Thomas Seminary in Denver, eight years at St. John's Seminary in Camarillo, California, and twelve years at Aquinas Institute of Theology in St. Louis.

Dan taught hundreds of students to preach, who now serve as bishops, priests, deacons, and lay ecclesial ministers across the United States and worldwide. Their preaching ministry, in turn, now testifies to the discipline, commitment, and devotion that Dan Harris brought to his Christian vocation as a Vincentian priest and teacher. I like to think of Dan's students paying the Gospel forward in their preaching ministry.

Dan began to describe himself as old in his sixties, and he visibly became more physically challenged. Dan died on January 28, 2016, at the age of 67. He had undergone minor surgery, and his body failed to thrive during the following days.

At Aquinas Institute of Theology, we learned of our colleague's death as we gathered around the altar to celebrate Eucharist on the feast of our patron, St. Thomas Aquinas. By coincidence, our school's ten-year reaccreditation visit by the Association of Theological Schools had finished that morning. We had planned to continue our celebration after Mass at a Mexican restaurant down the block. We did so—knowing that Dan would have appreciated our adding the completion of his life's mission to our celebration.

Now, over six years since Dan's death, I imagine he would be delighted that his Western Province of the Congregation of the Mission has relocated its Vincentian provincial offices to an entire floor of Aquinas Institute of Theology's urban building. Together, we Dominicans and Vincentians hope to tell a new story of collaboration and community engagement out of a shared sense of Gospel mission for preaching, theological education, and solidarity with those who suffer poverty and injustice. An attentive memory to Dan Harris and his life as a preacher and teacher can only inspire such collaboration, and I pray that Dan intercedes to God on our behalf.

This volume celebrates Dan Harris, the preacher. We found 283 Sunday and daily homily manuscripts on his school computer when he died. These included a relatively complete collection of his Sunday preaching from 2006 to 2007 at Sacred Heart Parish in Valley Park, Missouri, and from 2010 to 2011 at St. Catherine Labouré Parish in St. Louis. We know that during his twelve years at St. John's Seminary in Camarillo, California, Dan also preached regularly at Holy Cross Catholic Community in Moorpark under the founding pastorate of Fr. Joseph Cosgrove. Unfortunately, however, we do not have a record from Dan of that body of preaching.

While the manuscripts printed here with the permission of the Vincentians represent only a tiny percentage of Dan's years of preaching, they open a window into Dan's ministerial soul. In the following homilies, we have gathered twenty-four sample homilies to show one year of Advent, Christmas, Lent, and Easter preaching as heard at Sacred Heart and St. Catherine Labouré Parishes. We also have included five Sunday feasts in Ordinary Time, five Bread of Life homilies in Ordinary Time, and five homilies from other settings in which Dan preached: Aquinas Institute of Theology, the Sisters of Loretto at Nerinx High School, and the Vincentian Lazarist Residence. These beautifully written sermons required virtually no correction or editing for publication. We now leave our readers to imagine Dan bringing these words to life in the pulpit. We hope these homilies will challenge Dan's readers to live the Christian life and proclaim the gospel with a similar measure of his devotion and joy. To do so will be a fitting tribute to Dan Harris's memory.

Dan's body is buried in the Vincentian plot at Resurrection Cemetery in St. Louis. When I first visited his grave, I rejoiced to hear the bells of Kenrick-Glennon Seminary, where Dan taught for so many years, but I also was startled to see how small a grave is. How, in the end, does a whole life translate to so few square feet of real estate?

I have asked two of Dan's Vincentian confreres to say something about his life. Fr. Anthony J. Dosen, in his role as Mission Officer for the Congregation of the Mission, Western Province, knew Dan well. He writes obituaries for his confreres and knows his way around the Vincentian archives. I have asked Tony to give a brief biographical account of Dan's life, especially in the context of the Vincentian mission.

Fr. James Cormack has been the pastor of St. Catherine Laboure Parish in St. Louis for over twenty years. In 1995, during his prior pastorate at St. Vincent DePaul Parish in St. Louis, Jim was the first recipient of Aquinas Institute of Theology's annual Great Preacher Award. I have asked Jim to reflect on Dan's preaching ministry more personally as a Vincentian friend and parish pastor.

I owe a debt of thanks to Aquinas Scholar Emmanuel Diaz for the invaluable assistance by which this collection of essays and sermons became possible. When I asked Emmanuel to assist in organizing Dan's digital sermons to be given to the Vincentian archives, he suggested the selection of sermons chosen in this volume to represent a year of Dan Harris's preaching. Emmanuel has written introductions for each liturgical season and the three-point introduction for each homily according to season, text, and pastoral context. The homilies have been edited only to correct typos and remove Dan's Roman numeral section numbers. Dan wrote for the ear, and we left Dan's oral/aural voice intact. Emmanuel, a beginning Aquinas Institute Master of Divinity student, did not know Dan Harris personally. However, I like to think that Manny became one of Dan's students by organizing the homilies and discussing them with me.

Dan, as you live in happy memory, we can only imagine now the fullness of your Resurrection joy. Thank you for your life and ministry.

Daniel Harris, Vincentian

Anthony J. Dosen, CM

Fr. Dan Harris was born on March 24, 1946, one of six children of Mr. George William Harris and Mary Louise Pond, in Kankakee, Illinois, a small community about sixty miles south of Chicago. In Kankakee, Dan attended St. Patrick's Catholic School. When his family moved to Elgin, Illinois, in 1963, Dan transferred to Bishop McNamara High School. He completed his senior year at St. Edward's High School in Elgin, where he graduated in 1964. These were the high-water days of Catholic education when enrollments in Catholic schools were at all-time highs, thanks to the baby boom. The schools were staffed mainly by communities of sisters, brothers, and priests.

After graduating high school, Dan entered the novitiate of the Clerics of St. Viator in September 1964, and he remained with the Viatorians until 1969. After completing the novitiate, Dan studied theology at Loyola University in Chicago, following in the footsteps of his older brother, Fr. George Harris, CSV. While at Loyola, Dan encountered the popular theology professor, Fr. John Powell, SJ, one of the top spiritual writers of the 1960s and 70s. Dan found in Powell an example of how to engage students in the classroom—a lesson that was not lost when Dan began teaching homiletics after ordination. While at Loyola, Dan continued to discern his vocation to the Viatorians and the priesthood. When he withdrew from the Viatorians, Dan thought of being a priest of the Archdiocese of Chicago. However, his heart led him back to the communal life, and he chose the Vincentians.

Dan was a gregarious person, yet he had a private side. When speaking about his call to the Vincentians, he quipped that the Vincentian vocation director was the most persuasive. He also said it is not as important why one enters as why one stays in community. Dan's life certainly gave testimony of his dedication to the Congregation of the Mission, his apostolate of preaching and teaching preaching, and his shared life with his confreres.

Dan entered the Congregation of the Mission as a seminarian and later as a vowed member. He matriculated to DeAndreis Seminary in Lemont, Illinois, in the fall of 1969. Dan entered the novitiate in 1970 after a year of studies and then returned to DeAndreis Seminary to complete studies for ordination. He took vows at DeAndreas on June 5, 1972, and received ordination to the diaconate and priesthood over the subsequent two years.

While studying at DeAndreis, Dan was attracted to preaching under the influence of his preaching professor, Fr. Oscar Miller, CM. Miller taped the preaching of each student using videotaping technology of 1960s vintage that played to a portable black and white television. By today's standards, it was primitive, but it was cutting edge in Catholic preaching education in the late 1960s and 70s. When Fr. Dan's attraction to preaching and teaching homiletics led him to ask permission to pursue a master's degree in communications, the Vincentians sent him to study at the University of Southern California.

Completing his studies at USC in 1975, Dan was assigned to teach homiletics at Kenrick Seminary in St. Louis from 1975 to 1981. During those early years, he began to perfect his craft as both preacher and teacher.

Dan's second assignment was to DeAndreis Seminary in Lemont, Illinois, where he continued to teach homiletics using some of the same video equipment he had used as a student. During this time, I had Fr. Dan as my homiletics professor. My classmates and I were on our deacon internship and were required to send four homilies to Fr. Dan—a cassette tape, script, and evaluations from a select number of congregants. When he sent feedback, his comments were very helpful as we began our preaching ministry. As a student, I especially appreciated Fr. Dan's easy communication and engagement in and outside of class. He embodied the spirit of the Vincentians.

When DeAndreis Seminary closed in 1984, the Vincentian seminarians moved to St. Thomas Seminary in Denver. Dan moved there, as well, to develop the homiletics program. For the next two years at St. Thomas, he faithfully continued to do what had quickly become his life's work. Dan then returned to Kenrick-Glennon Seminary in St. Louis to teach preaching to seminarians and permanent deacon candidates for the next ten years.

To be closer to his mom, Mary Louise, who had moved to Las Vegas in her later years, Dan eventually asked to teach at St. John's Seminary in

Camarillo, California. While serving at St. John's, he renovated the seminary's preaching laboratory into a state-of-the-art facility.

In 1993, Dan enrolled in the Doctor of Ministry in Preaching program at Aquinas Institute of Theology in St. Louis, which he completed while teaching at Kenrick and St. John's, graduating with his advanced degree in 1998. Bishop Ken Untener was on Dan's thesis committee, with Aquinas Institute New Testament professor Mary Margaret Pazdan, OP, Dan's adviser. His thesis was titled "We Speak the Word of Life: A Self-Directed Continuing Education and Formation Resource for Preachers."

Upon completion of his term at St. John's, Fr. Dan joined the homiletics faculty at Aquinas Institute, teaching seminarians, lay Master of Divinity students, and seasoned Catholic and Protestant preachers in the nation's only Catholic doctoral program in preaching. Along with his teaching, Fr. Dan spoke at clergy development days and other ongoing formation programs throughout the United States, Europe, and the South Pacific. He also gave preaching workshops for the National Organization for Continuing Education of Roman Catholic Clergy (NOCERCC). Additionally, he published two books and various articles on preaching and preaching education.

His accomplishments in the field of Catholic homiletics only underscore the whimsical and delightful human being, priest, and Vincentian that Fr. Dan Harris was. Even now, one can only smile thinking of this cigar-smoking, smiling, quick-witted Dan and his love of life and love of people. The office staff at St. John's Seminary in Camarillo looked forward to sitting with Dan as he held court at lunch each day. We Vincentians whom he had taught and with whom he lived fondly remember Dan's joyful presence in our common life. Perhaps this was the secret of his homiletic wisdom: he knew and loved people. He wanted to share with them the gift he had received, the *Kerygma*, the Good News, "God loves us!"

Dan Harris was born during the early days of the baby boom after World War II. He attended Catholic schools during the 1950s and early 60s, a time of unbridled growth, new confidence for Catholicism in the United States, and fertile ground for a vocation to the priesthood. His brother, nine years older than Dan, was a Viatorian. Dan studied under the magnetic influence of the Jesuits at Loyola University. He also considered becoming an archdiocesan priest in Chicago. Yet, Dan joined the Vincentians! Fr. Daniel Harris, CM, chose to spend his life and ministry in a community dedicated to bringing the gospel to the poor. Early in his formation as a Vincentian, he decided to devote himself to the art of preaching and teaching preaching. Dan was one of us, and he shared his knowledge, warmth, and life with us.

On January 28, 2016, on the Feast of St. Thomas Aquinas, preacher, teacher, philosopher, theologian, and mystic, Fr. Dan returned to the God who made him, called him, and graced us all by allowing him to be a part of our lives.

> *This essay includes archival data from the Provincial Archive of the Congregation of the Mission, Western Province; the DeAndreis-Rosati Memorial Archives, DePaul University, Chicago, Illinois; and the Provincial Archives of the Clerics of St. Viator, Arlington Heights, Illinois.*

Dan Harris, Parish Preacher

James Cormack, CM

There are many opinions about what makes a good preacher a good preacher. Tell stories, tell jokes, keep it short, keep it real, keep yourself out of it, and make it approachable enough, but there are many more suggestions about preaching well. Most fundamental: Love your people, your congregation, your fellow travelers on the way to the kingdom. Know them as best you can, respect them, care about them, and want what is right for them, best for them. Since preaching is telling the story of God's love for us, it must be grounded in a healthy personality, a growing person, someone who loves God, someone who knows their need for God's mercy and forbearance, God's faithfulness, the mystery of God's being with us in Christ Jesus, yet wholly beyond us in majesty. The maker of us all, the source of our very being, and the One we long to know and love more fully.

Good psychology and good spirituality are not just similar; they are the same truth told with different words. A good preacher is a good person, a good friend. That was Dan Harris.

I knew Dan best when we lived and were formed together in our seminary days. One might be damning another with faint praise to say he was good. But live long enough, and you will discover that beyond the superlatives one might gain by way of talent and skill, being recognized as good goes to character, which is powerfully more important. We believers know that one who is good is full of grace, not earned but instead received, accepted, and gratefully implemented. It is a life's task and goal to be good, full of grace, never fully accomplished, but faithfully acknowledged and embraced daily. Good preaching rests upon the bedrock of good character. It is foundational; it is centering; it is demanding; it is preaching's fullest reward. We together grow in holiness, better said, in grace. Together we become more fully alive in the mystery and power of God's love. So again, Dan Harris was a good person, a good friend, a good man, a good priest, a good Vincentian, someone who had something good to say, from the very store of God's goodness. Who wouldn't want to listen to him? Preaching requires technique and practice, but it depends upon goodness, better said Grace.

Now that I have set him up for canonization, let me assure you he was no paper-mâché saint. Impish comes to mind, zany, able to see the absurd and enjoy it, funny in a surely demented way. He was insightful and incisive, happy to recognize his superior understanding compared to yours. He was inquisitive about human nature and human fallibility and could manage a well-developed sarcasm about the infinite capacity of we humans to be foolish.

Humor was a close friend of his. Back in the 1970s, he loved Monty Python and Dr. Demento. His palate for humor was that of a gourmand. While he could pun with the best, he instead demanded educated humor. He was willing to acknowledge the value of attempting this high-achievement humor even if the attempt was not funny. Good preaching doesn't need good jokes (they are hard to find). It does require someone with a good sense of humor, about oneself, our fallible church, our broken yet wondrous world, and life itself. Humor that teaches most of life is ordinary, occasioned by crisis, but rarely critical, and wondrous even in its most challenging moments if we have eyes to see God at work with care, insight, and depth in all and every moment.

Dan had a good sense of humor. He loved God, and God's people, whom he took very seriously; himself, not so much. And so people would say, "He speaks to me," and, "He makes a living the faith something very real." He often was jocular as a way to be approachable. He always gathered the congregation together to pursue holiness and reminded us that this pursuit was noble and absolutely necessary. Growing in grace wasn't a chore, though it always demands our very best. Growing in grace was an opportunity, a quest about growing fully alive, something that would leave you tired but happy. A glow comes from responding to our baptismal call not as a life sentence but instead as life's purpose. Dan preached in such a way as to encourage us to take the plunge into something not only greater, but something only God could give, and to which eventually nothing could compare. God loves you. Open your eyes, mind, and heart to this; it will ask your all, and if you enter into it, it will make you more. Inviting our response to God's love is the mark of a good preacher, a good man, a wise man, a grace-filled man.

Dan was a Vincentian, a member of the Congregation of the Mission founded in seventeenth-century France by St. Vincent de Paul, founded so that the poor might have the good news preached to them. And so, he knew how essential preaching the just word was. And no, the just word is not the "liberal agenda." The Gospel of Jesus Christ, the Word of God, sent by the Father, addresses both liberals and conservatives, so we might know and live God's faithful love, justice, and true peace. The just word is the wisdom and power of our Scriptures, and the one who preaches the just word is tasked with making it no less alive and real now than when it was spoken and heard so long ago.

I'm sure you have experienced a browbeating, a stinging self-righteous rant from the pulpit under the guise of preaching the just word. That is not good preaching; it is not the just word. It was never Dan Harris. It wasn't just that he knew you draw more flies with honey than with vinegar. It was because he loved and cared for those to whom he preached that he knew how to invite and challenge, to correct and cajole with God's word, all the while encouraging not only conversion but also a willingness to build the kingdom of peace and justice together. Dan would ask us, fellow pilgrims on the way, growing in our understanding and commitment to the world transformed by the presence and power of the One who emptied himself on the wood of the Cross for us all, to embrace the mission of transformation joyfully. To find the fullness of life, we die to ourselves to live for one another and live in God's image and likeness. The just word Dan preached was not only the good news; it was compelling; it was life-giving. People would respond, saying to themselves, yes, I want to live that truth, I want to be a partner in this transforming truth, this new heaven and new earth in which God's justice and love reigns.

And my final observation, Dan helped those he preached to want more. We Christians believe in the resurrection of the dead and life everlasting. We grow more fully alive as we encounter this mystery. There is more. As wondrous as life can be, it is never full here. Our love is never complete, our happiness unending. When we grow fully alive in the fullness of life, we come to when God calls us home, and then the journey is complete. Our wanting more empowers us to do the hard work of loving, forgiving, hoping, looking for, and finding the good, God's grace in us, among us, and all around us. Dan could offer the comfort only our faith in the resurrection could provide and fulfill. Be glad for what you are, long for the fullness of God's life to grow in you, want more to become more, to grow up until you have outgrown growth, reaping the fruit of God's sweet harvest. Life is changed, not ended, so be courageous and bold, live life with all its messiness and clumsiness, heartbreak, and danger. The One who has made you has plans for you that no evil or deprivation can destroy. Believe and Live. Dan Harris preached this not only with words but also with his life, wisdom, humor, and faith.

Daniel Harris, Seminary Preaching Teacher

Gregory Heille, OP

Dan Harris simply loved to teach preaching, and he did so for forty-two years. He taught countless seminarians preparing for ordination and directed the thesis projects of thirteen Doctor of Ministry in Preaching students.[1] In addition to his doctoral thesis, he wrote two books. He also spoke and consulted widely as the guest of dioceses, religious communities, and seminaries. Dan's confreres, colleagues, and students knew him as a wonderful man, a gifted preacher, a master teacher, and an important figure in American Catholic homiletics.

Philosophy of Teaching

In 2011, Dan wrote a three-page teaching philosophy. He wrote:

> I approach teaching as a learning-centered enterprise. A teacher-centered approach is based on methods and strategies with which a teacher might feel most comfortable. A student-centered approach is planned around the way particular students in a class might prefer to learn. Since a class is not primarily about the comfort of teachers or students, the learning-centered strategy asks both teacher and student to focus on the reason we are gathered: to learn.

Dan took a learning-centered approach to teaching with respect, humor, and individual attention to his students. He intentionally modeled

---

1. Deacon David J. Shea, Rev. Jon Good, Fr. Kevin Huber, Fr. Eddie De Leon ,CMF, Rev. Daniel Defassio, Fr. Jeff Harvey, CM, Fr. Michael Nolan, Fr. Louis Guerin, Dr. Karla Bellinger, Dr. Suzanne Nawrocki, Fr. Shane Crombie, Fr. Alex Zenthoefer, and Dr. Sharon Schuhmann.

respect and humor so that these qualities would make their way into his students' preaching. In the statement of his teaching philosophy, he wrote:

> I am especially interested in modeling respect in the homiletics classroom since future preachers will need to extend that same respect to their congregations. Even if a preacher needs to present a strong prophetic message, it must be done with great sensitivity and respect for the congregation.
>
> I believe strongly that learning takes place when we are relaxed, and most our natural selves. That often involves good natured laughter. I often use humor in my own preaching in a strategic way. . . . When we laugh, we relax and let down our defenses. And that, in turn, allows us the freedom to take in a difficult message.

Dan appeared to never tire of meeting individually with his students to do a rubric-based review and talk about their preaching. Each preaching was camcorded and played back on a small television on his office desk. Dan loved to keep up to date with technology. Before his death, one of his major projects was designing state-of-the-art preaching lab classrooms—including the Homiletics and Liturgy Training Center at St. John's Seminary in Camarillo, California, and the Delaplane Preaching Studio of Aquinas Institute of Theology in St. Louis. In his teaching philosophy, Dan traced this interest to his teacher, Oscar Miller, CM:

> When I was a seminarian I had a homiletics teacher, Oscar Miller, CM, who was something of a pioneer in Catholic homiletics education. He was one of the first to record student preaching in the classroom (using a state-of-the-art wire audio recorder). By the time I studied with him, he was using reel-to-reel videotape. His teaching was innovative in a day when many seminaries had no trained homiletics teachers. I learned a great deal from him about teaching. The most important thing he taught me was to spend time with each student individually.

Dan's teaching over many years at Kenrick-Glennon Seminary impacted two generations of priests throughout the Archdiocese of St. Louis, including Fr. Mitch Doyen, pastor of St. John the Baptist Parish in South St. Louis. When asked to reflect on his two years of preaching courses at Kenrick-Glennon Seminary from 1988 to 1990, Mitch remembered frequent one-on-one appointments in which Dan critiqued Mitch's preaching and showed an interest in his faith journey. "Dan had a profound respect for each one of us. I liked his soothing, gentle voice and soft-spoken sense of humor. Dan connected, and it was evident that he cared. Dan was humble, and he did not take himself too seriously. He didn't want us to take ourselves too seriously, either. He encouraged us to be pastoral in our approach to preaching."

Calling the preaching life an adventure, Mitch describes his preaching preparation process: "Every Monday afternoon, I submit a church bulletin article on the Sunday readings. First, I read the text and consult the Sunday Web Site at Saint Louis University. My preaching percolates all week until I see my homily as a series of scenes, like in a movie. I keep an index card in my pocket, a list of the scenes. My preaching is not text or notes-bound but conversational. The Word is living, and I long to honor the encounter taking place in the Assembly. I want to explain what I saw, not tell people what I think. I want to break open the Word and prompt an encounter with Christ."

At Aquinas Institute of Theology beginning in 2004, Dan taught the Foundations of Preaching course over two semesters to follow the seasons of the liturgical year: Advent, Christmas, Lent, and Easter. He also taught advanced preaching courses according to topics of his choice, including Doctrinal Preaching, Preaching in the Public Square, and Preaching in an Age of New Media. In the summers, Dan taught in Aquinas Institute's popular Summer Preaching Institute, where church ministers from across the country studied over three summers for two weeks each June to earn a graduate certificate in preaching. Dan also team-taught the Core Homiletic Seminars in Aquinas Institute's unique Doctor of Ministry in Preaching program. In these advanced courses, ordained and lay church ministers studied the best of homiletic literature, brought their video-recorded preaching for collegial critique, and prepared to do thesis research.

Once, when Dan's beginner students in preaching weren't doing their reading, he required them to post comments and questions about the readings before class. In his teaching philosophy, Dan confessed:

> I told the students this process would help me have a better sense of their issues before I taught the class. A little deception is important in good teaching. However, this strategy became a self-fulfilling prophecy. I am much better prepared to teach class as a result of reading their comments and questions before we meet. At times they have asked questions that required a bit of research on my part. The one-day notice allowed me to be better prepared to address their concerns. This experience taught me that I am never a finished product as a teacher. Although our academic dean refers

to me as a "most seasoned teacher" I still have much to learn about this noble craft; and I hope to keep learning.

We Speak the Word of the Lord

Dan showed little interest in pursuing an academic rank above that of an assistant professor. However, he diligently pursued a doctoral degree in his field, becoming one of the first Aquinas Institute of Theology Doctor of Ministry in Preaching graduates. His 1998 thesis on "We Speak the Word of Life: A Self-Directed Continuing Education and Formation Resource for Preachers" was directed by New Testament scholar Mary Margaret Pazdan, OP, and Bishop Kenneth Untener.

In 2001, he published *We Speak the Word of the Lord: A Practical Plan for More Effective Preaching*. Now available in a 2012 reprint edition, this text will be familiar to many of Dan's students. The table of contents indicates Dan's comprehensive understanding of his topic:

1. What is a Homily? Do We Preach Christ, or Preach *about* Christ?
2. Making a Homily Outstanding: Can Every Homily be Outstanding?
3. Creating a Homily: Telling the Old Story in a Fresh Way
4. Preaching the Scriptures: Do We Preach *on* God's Word of *from* God's Word?
5. The Preacher's Own Faith: "You will be my witnesses . . . " (Acts 1:8)
6. Listening to the Listeners: How Do Preachers Include Other Voices?
7. Preaching the Prophetic Word: Offering a New Imagination
8. Daily Homilies, Funerals, Weddings: Preaching on Weekdays and Special Occasions[2]

In 1990, Dan had published an earlier version of the book, written with Edward Murphy, CM, who had taught preaching at Kenrick Seminary in St. Louis.[3] Dan's photo on the back cover showed a young, bearded Dan Harris who already had been teaching preaching for thirteen years. As the cover bio indicates, Dan was already deeply involved in the continuing formation of preachers as a visiting professor at All Hallows Seminary in

---

2. Harris, *We Speak the Word of the Lord*, 3.
3. Harris and Murphy, *Overtaken by the Word*.

Dublin and St. Vincent de Paul Regional Seminary in Florida and founder of the Vincentian Preaching Workshops.

Though the tables of contents of the 1990 and 2001 books were somewhat similar, Dan rewrote each chapter in line with current homiletic scholarship. In doing so, he made his priorities clear. In a section on first and second-order language in the first chapter, Dan emphasized the importance of "preaching Christ" through the personal witness of faith rather than by a more removed "preaching about Christ." He described this approach to preaching as an encounter: "Preaching is not so much talking about God as it is a personal encounter among God, the congregation and the preacher."[4] Today, preaching students can relate to this kerygmatic understanding of preaching as testimony and a call to transforming encounter. Dan offered this definition of the homily: "A homily is a preaching event that is integral to the liturgy to proclaim the saving mystery of God in the scriptures. It calls and empowers the hearers to faith, a deeper participation in the Eucharist, and daily discipleship to Christ lived out in the church."[5]

We Speak the Word of the Lord includes an excellent chapter on prophetic preaching that bears the marks of Old Testament scholar Walter Brueggemann's work on prophetic preaching as reimagination. Dan wrote:

> Authentic prophetic preaching offers an alternate imagination filled with hope. . . . Part of the process of offering a new imagination involves the uncomfortable task of dismantling those dimensions of religiosity that no longer allow God to be God. . . . Jesus is the ultimate dismantler of the old static religion and the politics of oppression."[6]

Dan offered six guidelines for preaching the prophetic word:[7]

Preach God and Nothing Less.

Preach for Change.

Preach As One Who Lives Justice.

Preach with Compassion.

Preach to the Whole Church.

Preach Hope.

---

4. Harris, *We Speak the Word of the Lord*, 19.
5. Harris, *We Speak the Word of the Lord*, 24.
6. Harris, *We Speak the Word of the Lord*, 146–7.
7. Harris, *We Speak the Word of the Lord*, 154–5.

His paragraph on preaching for change was particularly indicative of his future collaboration with homiletician Ray John Marek, OMI, on preaching in the public square:

> Biblical prophets preached conversion. Contemporary social justice preaching not only names the sin in the community, it offers the power to imagine a new just world. Burghardt calls preachers to proclaim the just word in a way that calls for action. Effective social justice preaching moves listeners to identify the justice issues in their midst, discover what resources they have to address these issues and develop concrete plans of action.[8]

Since shortly after publication, Dan's book has been a preaching textbook at St. Vincent de Paul Regional Seminary in Boynton Beach, Florida. Dan had taught reaching at the seminary as a visiting professor, and several alumni have shared how good a professor he was.

In 2007, the seminary hired Dan as a consultant to assist with a reaccreditation project to make homiletics a focus of quality improvement for the seminary. Dan visited twice to help the seminary envision its homiletics curriculum and goals. When Dan died, a third visit was scheduled.

Monsignor Stephen Bosso of the St. Vincent de Paul faculty remembers Dan's insights as invaluable:

> His style was vintage Dan Harris—never judgmental, always encouraging, challenging, but with a good sense of humor so that you looked forward to conversations with him. He was always positive with the intent to build up the program and, more importantly, the folks of the faculty and administration. Dan was a steady hand and guiding light full of insights, experience, education, and strong faith in Jesus Christ that wanted to see Jesus Christ preached. I got a distinct impression that Dan took our project very personally. You see, the Vincentians founded St. Vincent de Paul Regional Seminary. They ran the seminary for its initial eight years before withdrawing and turning over the seminary to the Archdiocese of Miami.

Homiletics remains a significant part of St. Vincent de Paul's Master of Divinity and Master of Arts in Theological Studies programs. Dan's spirit has lived on in the four preaching professors sent for doctoral study at Aquinas Institute of Theology: Fr. Louis Guerin, Msgr. Stephen Bosso, Fr. Gregg Caggianelli, and Fr. Bryan Garcia.

---

8. Harris, *We Speak the Word of the Lord*. 154.

Renewing Sunday Preaching

Dan enjoyed presenting preaching workshops for clergy and laity and was proud to have been a guest lecturer at St. Vincent de Paul Regional Seminary in Boynton Beach, All Hallows College in Dublin, the North American College in Rome, and the Diocese of Samoa-Pago Pago in American Samoa. In 1988 and 1999, Dan served the Catholic Association of Teachers of Homiletics (CATH) as vice president and then president. He also was a consultor and contributor to Saint Meinrad Seminary and School of Theology's video series *Preaching for Today and Tomorrow* and a writer for the CATH white paper on criteria for certification of homiletics teachers and curriculum development for Roman Catholic seminaries.

Dan participated in Catholic Coalition on Preaching and Academy of Homiletics conferences. He also participated in two grant projects funded by the Wabash Center for Teaching and Learning in Theology and Religion in Indiana. These included a 2004 consultation on biblical preaching at Aquinas Institute of Theology and a 2008 consultation on teaching homiletics at the Wabash Center. In the book resulting from the Wabash Center consultation, Dan contributed a comprehensive chapter on assessing student preaching, including several rubrics.[9]

In 2001, the National Association for Continuing Education of Roman Catholic Clergy (NOCERCC, now known as the Association for the Ongoing Formation of Priests) launched its Renewing Sunday Preaching convocation program for diocesan and religious order bishops, priests, and deacons who preach at Sunday Eucharist. Dan Harris participated in numerous two-member convocation teams—in Belleville, Illinois; Salina, Kansas; Sacramento, California; and elsewhere.

As indicated in NOCERCC's unpublished Renewing Sunday Preaching handbook,

> The Priestly Life and Ministry Committee of the NCCB [had] identified the improved Sunday Preaching as a principal goal, while The Catholic Coalition on Preaching, a cooperation among 16 national organizations (NOCERCC being one of them), was working toward a coordinated, national effort to effect real improvement in the state of Catholic preaching. In 1999 a symposium was held and it resulted in a call for just such a priestly convocation. NOCERCC convened a special committee of continuing education/formation

---

9. Harris, "Methods of Assessment."

directors and theologian-priests to respond to that call, and the *Renewing Sunday Preaching* program was created.

Each gathering included four two-hour presentations, with talks, video material, handouts, and discussion exercises. The former NOCERCC website described the four sessions as follows:

- *Preaching—the Agony and the Ecstasy* Participants see and hear lay people speaking of the importance of preaching for them and are invited to share their own experiences of preaching.
- *Preacher: Namer, Interpreter, Reflector* Three images of the preacher are considered in light of the coming Sunday's readings: namer of grace, interpreter of the Bible, and theological reflector.
- *Catholic Vision of Homily* A Catholic vision of the Sunday homily leads to naming the abilities, skills, and knowledge needed for inspiring and effective preaching.
- *Preaching Resources* Methods of integrating preaching preparation and the minister's life in a spirituality of the preacher and basic resources to support the preacher are suggested.

Preaching in the Public Square

In 2001, Dan began a forward-looking collaboration with Ray John Marek, OMI, called "A Public Voice: Preaching on Justice Issues" and also referred to as "The Public Square Project." Dan then taught preaching at St. John's Seminary in Camarillo and Ray John at Oblate School of Theology in San Antonio. This grant-funded project originated in the Catholic Study Group of the Public Character of Theological Education Project of the Association of Theological Schools in the United States and Canada.

Dan and Ray John published a comprehensive project description in the ATS journal *Theological Education*. They asked: "How might a student preacher be motivated to begin developing his or her 'public character' as a minister of the Word in a world needing the Gospel infused with justice?"[10] The Public Square Project responded to this question by developing four modules for preaching classrooms.

- Preaching Biblical Justice

10. Marek and Harris, "Preaching on Justice Issues," 47.

- Preaching the Prophetic Word
- Justice Preaching: The Development of Public Character
- Interpreting People's Lives in Light of God's Just Word

Each module was to include discussion questions and activities, along with video interviews and recorded preaching by five Catholic social justice preachers: Fr. Doug Doussan, a New Orleans pastor and co-founder of the local Pax Christi chapter; Fr. Lou Arceneaux, CM, another New Orleans pastor and a regular participant in the "Justfaith" religious television broadcast; Fr. David Garcia, rector of San Fernando Cathedral Parish in San Antonio and a staff member for Catholic Relief Services; Msgr. Jim Telthorst, a St. Louis pastor and authority on preaching and the liturgy; and Fr. Perry Henry, CM, the pastor of St. Joseph's Catholic Church in New Orleans who had been active in resettling the poor and the homeless after Hurricane Katrina.

Unfortunately, even after much work, Dan had not completed the video production for the four Public Square modules when he died. Much of the video work was lost, and the materials were not distributed to homiletics teachers as intended. However, the intention of forming preachers to preach the social gospel according to the signs of the times remains timely. I encourage teachers of preaching to keep in mind the following key insights which are described in the four modules of the Public Square Project:

- Biblical justice is more inclusive than Western notions of justice.
- Authentic prophetic preaching is different from mere moralism.
- Every preaching event can make room for a hermeneutic of justice.
- The homily does not so much explain scripture as interpret life in light of the scripture.[11]

The Performance of Joy

Dan once wrote, "Preaching, like poetry, is a sacred word in the oral/aural world that is intended to be performative. The preached word is less about explaining God and far more about inviting the believer to meet the Lord

---

11. Marek and Harris, "Preaching on Justice Issues," 49–50.

in the sacrament of the spoken word."[12] In his humor, faith, and lasting commitment to preaching and teaching preaching, Dan's life was an accomplished performance of the Gospel.

Perhaps no official document of the Catholic Church speaks more cogently about the ministry of the Word and homiletic preaching than Pope Francis's 2013 apostolic exhortation, *The Joy of the Gospel*. The exhortation takes its name from its first sentences:

> The joy of the gospel fills the hearts and lives of all who encounter Jesus. Those who accept his offer of salvation are set free from sin, sorrow, inner emptiness and loneliness. With Christ joy is constantly born anew. In this Exhortation I wish to encourage the Christian faithful to embark upon a new chapter of evangelization marked by this joy, while pointing out new paths for the Church's journey in years to come.[13]

For Pope Francis, evangelization is a performance of discipleship marked by joy. Like Dan's preaching and teaching, Dan Harris's life was such an act of evangelization—a performance of discipleship marked by joy.

Bibliography

Francis. Apostolic Exhortation *Evangelii Gaudium* (2013). www.vatican.va.
Harris, Daniel E. "Methods of Assessment." In *Teaching Preaching as a Christian Practice: A New Approach to Homiletic Pedagogy*, edited by Thomas G. Long and Leonora Tubbs Tisdale, 191–204. Louisville: Westminster John Knox, 2008.
———. *We Speak the Word of the Lord: A Practical Plan for More Effective Preaching*. Chicago: ACTA, 2001. Reprint, Eugene: Wipf and Stock, 2012.
Harris, Daniel E., and Edward F. Murphy. *Overtaken by the Word: The Theology and Practice of Preaching*. Denver: Rubicon, 1990.
Marek, Ray John, and Daniel E. Harris. "A Public Voice: Preaching on Justice Issues." *Theological Education* 38:1 (2001) 47–59.
Signatures. Aquinas Institute of Theology Newsletter (2011).

---

12. Harris, *Signatures*.
13. *Evangelii Gaudium* 1.

Preaching Through the Liturgical Year
by Daniel Harris, CM

EDITED BY
Emmanuel Diaz

Advent

F<small>R. D</small>AN'S A<small>DVENT</small> H<small>OMILIES</small> had a twofold purpose. The first was to prepare for the coming of Christ in history, in grace, and in the fullness of time; the second was to remind the community that even if the approaching Christmas season can be an emotional burden for families and loved ones, it also is a time of joy. Dan interpreted the first readings to highlight the Jewish people's great anticipation for the coming of the Messiah. In the gospels, Dan saw John the Baptist as a role model for receiving Christ and following him as disciples.

Dan often described the great joy of Christ's arrival to the world while empathizing with those who felt distant from God and missed their deceased loved ones in the holiday season. Recognizing our universal call to discipleship, Dan challenged the community to be supportive and loving towards those in the community who are in pain. Ultimately, Christ desires to enter our suffering world to share his peace, leading us to joy in eternal life with God.

1st Sunday of Advent, Year B

Sacred Heart Parish, Valley Park, Missouri

November 27, 2005

- **Season:** Advent is a season to celebrate three arrivals of Christ: Jesus's arrival in history at Bethlehem, his arrival here and now in grace, and his coming again at the end of the world to establish the kingdom of God fully.
- **Text:** As we consider our lives in terms of Isaiah's lamentation and hope, we see Advent as an especially opportune time to stay awake and guard for God's coming.

- **Pastoral Context:** As we meet Christ in the Eucharist during Advent, we can find our way as disciples amid our time's worldly materialism and complex ethical challenges.

Materialism and Violence I woke up the morning after Thanksgiving with the startling news on my radio. The shopping center parking lots were filling up quickly. With all of the important things going on throughout the world, the Friday news told stories about how retail sales are doing this season, how they will compare with last year, and whether this will be a successful Christmas season. The pre-Christmas news is also filled with stories of violence throughout the world and people who will have miserable Christmases because of recent natural disasters. How sad to think that we have almost a month of that to look forward to.

Christians are not Scrooges—most of us enjoy giving gifts and receiving them at Christmas. But in the midst of all that is going on in the world, if the most important part of our Christmas is what we buy and receive, we are missing the essence of this season.

Isaiah names the sin. I must be honest—I'm not genuinely depressed this morning. I was doing a little lamenting. Lamenting is a kind of biblical complaining about the present state of things. Biblical people lament when their lives are not going as they had hoped. The prophet Isaiah is doing some lamenting in the first reading this morning. Isaiah is writing at that very bleak time in Israel's history when the people return home after their captivity and exile in Babylon. They have finally been set free from their enemies, but they come home to a city in ruins. And they know that part of the sadness they feel has been brought on themselves through their own sins. They have wandered far from the Lord, and they lament that sin.

Isaiah names a solution. The prophet, however, does not wallow in self-pity over the sins of the people. There is a real ray of hope here contained in one three-letter word. That word is *yet*. After going on about how the people have strayed from God, how their lives are in ruins, and how they can't seem to get it together, the prophet says, and *yet* . . . "Yet, you Lord are our father, you are the potter, and we are the clay." In other words, God can reshape his people. God has the power to make them the kind of people he created them to be. There is hope.

Advent: Three Arrivals Hope is at the heart of Advent. This First Sunday of Advent is the beginning of the church's new liturgical year. Well, the new year is always a time for starting over. Don't people often make New Year's resolutions like losing weight or giving up smoking? In this church's new year, the resolution is far more important. In the spirit of this lament from Isaiah, the resolution is about beginning to walk in a new way. We want to walk in a new way because we are preparing to celebrate the birth of Jesus at Christmas. We celebrate that time in history when God came among us as a human. Actually, we celebrate three arrivals of Christ during Advent. In addition to celebrating Jesus's arrival in history at Bethlehem, we celebrate his arrival here and now in grace, and thirdly we celebrate our faith that Jesus will come again at the end of the world to fully establish the kingdom of God. Jesus was born in history, Jesus comes into our hearts now in grace, Jesus will come again. Three arrivals.

Gospel: Stay awake and on guard. Because Advent is about the Lord coming into our midst in these three ways, Jesus in the gospel tells us to stay awake—to be watchful. Jesus tells this story, a mini-parable really, about the master who goes away on a trip and places his servants in charge. But they must keep watchful because they don't know the time when the master will return. When Jesus says, you don't know the *time* of the return, the scriptures use the Greek word *kairos*. This is significant. If I want to say that the time is 9:30 AM or 11:00 AM, I would use the Greek word *chronos*, not *kairos*. So what? It makes a big difference. *Kairos* means that this time, this moment, is finally "my time." "My ship has come in." This is my big moment. If I am late for a 9:00 AM *chronos* appointment, I can just change my schedule a bit to rearrange things. But if it is *kairos* time and my ship has come in, there might not be another ship. I have to be ready. And so, we must always be ready for the Lord in our lives. This is big stuff. Stay on guard, Jesus says. In the Roman army, if a soldier fell asleep during guard duty, he could be executed. That is harsh punishment, but a sleeping guard can allow an enemy to sneak into camp and kill everyone. Jesus uses that image to stress how urgent it is for us to be watchful.

Embryonic Stem Cells Being watchful for the second coming does not mean that we stand around gawking up at the sky looking for Jesus to return (gesture this). Being watchful means that we live every aspect of our day-in and day-out lives as people who know where we are heading. We are people created to join the Lord for all time. Along this day-in and day-out road, every so often there is a major public event that reminds us we live in a world among plenty of people who do not share our beliefs and values. This Sunday, the bishops of Missouri have asked that all priests and deacons address the upcoming petition campaign to eventually legalize embryonic stem cell research. If the group sponsoring this petition drive can collect 145,000 signatures, the issue will be on the ballot one year from now. This can be a confusing issue for serious Christians because we hear ads on the radio and TV that this research will result in many wonderful cures—and who can be against that?

The Issues for a Believer As believers who love the Lord, we are not against wonderful cures. Stem cells can reproduce in marvelous ways to cure diseases or even replace diseased organs. In fact, the Catholic Church fully supports stem cell research when the cells are obtained in ethical ways—such as from adult donors. The ethical issue in this new campaign is that it favors producing human life (embryonic life) solely to harvest these stem cells for research. Then the life is destroyed. Some well-meaning scientists see nothing wrong with that because they are thinking of the possible cures ahead. But a believer needs to say, "Wait a minute—we have just manufactured human life and then tossed it aside after we took those stem cells. Even if the motivation is a positive one, we can't treat human life that way. Human cloning also goes against our belief that our Lord is the author of life in that cloned humans become laboratory productions. As we begin this Advent, we hear our scriptures remind us where we came from and what our destiny is. One very practical way for us to express this faith is to let our legislators know that as believers, we see the real purpose of our lives. We are being called by our bishops to stand up and remind our brothers and sisters that the Lord is the sole author of life. There will be more to come on this topic later so that we can keep ourselves responsibly informed.

Eucharist Lord's Presence Now Meanwhile, we are in this Advent time of watchful waiting. We watch for Christmas when we celebrate Jesus's coming into our lives in history, we watch for Jesus on the last day, and today, right now, we watch for Jesus coming into our lives through his grace. He profoundly does that in this Eucharist—where we receive his body and blood.

2nd Sunday of Advent, Year A

St. Catherine Laboure Parish, St. Louis, Missouri

December 5, 2010

- **Season:** As we continue our Advent celebration, we can ask, "If the Lord is in our hearts, what could our world and our lives be like?"

- **Text:** Following Isaiah's vision of God's kingdom, John the Baptist gives us the formula for seeking a relationship with Jesus: turn away from sin and open our hearts to Christ the Messiah.
- **Pastoral Context:** In our hopes and prayers during Advent, we can constantly seek to grow closer to God and to know what God wants us to do.

The Lion and the Lamb Our first reading from the prophet Isaiah says a time will come when wild animals will live in harmony with children. I remember reading a story from way back in the days of the cold war—back when the Soviet Union and the United States had nuclear missiles aimed at one another in the 1960s. A Soviet propaganda officer was leading Western journalists on a tour of Moscow. They passed a cage in Red Square that held a lion and a lamb. The officer said, "This is an example of the peaceful coexistence we wish between our countries. When a journalist asked how these animals managed to get along so well, the propaganda officer said, "It has worked out perfectly." But a little old Russian man walking by added under his breath, "However, they must put a fresh lamb in the cage each morning." And that is the reality we know. The reading says that little children and wild animals will get along just fine. Come on, folks, this is a fairy tale; this ideal vision is impossible. And so it is in the world as we know it. We see the horrors of war and terrorism on TV as the war in Afghanistan drones on. Our own city of St. Louis recently was ranked as the most dangerous city in the United States per capita. We know a very violent world. So what is Isaiah talking about? Isaiah has a vision of the kingdom of God, of the way it can be. That is a major message of Advent that we continue to celebrate on this second Sunday. If the Lord is in our hearts, what could our world and our lives be like? How would the evening news look different; how would our own lives look different? This is the message from John the Baptist in today's gospel—a strange character in a long line of prophets.

John envisions a new world. John calls the people to turn away from their sins and open their hearts to Christ the Messiah—the savior. John looked at the way things were and gave people a vision of how things can be. Here is this guy living in the desert, wearing animal skins for clothing, eating locusts for lunch (eating bugs, for heaven's sake). While John may seem strange to us, the ancient people understood what his appearance meant. Long ago, the prophet Malachi looked at the state of his world and told the people in God's name that Elijah would return to set things right.

Elijah would wear strange clothes, eat strange foods, and most of all would announce that God's messiah was coming. Is John Elijah, returned? We do know that John came to announce that Jesus the Messiah, at last, is here.

Why did people flock to John? So why did people flock out into the desert to hear this man yell at them about repenting because the Messiah is coming? Could it be that after being let down by so many hypocritical religious leaders, after so much empty religion, the people were tired and ready for serious repentance? Did they maybe know that at last, this is the real article? This is the one who can help us set things right?

Revivals Maybe some came to hear John preach for the same reason that people flock to old-time revivals. There is lots of bombastic preaching and singing at an old-time revival. Mark Twain has a wonderful account of the time Tom Sawyer was in bed with the measles for weeks. While Tom was sick, the little Missouri town had a religious tent revival, but Tom Sawyer missed it all. Once Tom recovered, he was astounded at the change in people. Everyone was polite; merchants treated people fairly, and there was no smoking, drinking, or swearing. Tom hated every bit of it. He was the only normal person left. But to his delight, after only a few weeks, everything in town was back to normal. Twain was saying that these emotional revivals whip people into a frenzy, but it soon wears off. If that is what people expected from listening to John the Baptist, they were mistaken. He came to preach a deep-down genuine repentance. John was calling people to truly turn away from their former lives and be ready to accept Christ. John came to preach the way things could become for those who accept Christ.

What are my dreams? As we hear these scriptures today, we may ask ourselves, what are the dreams that we have for a better world? For a better me? If we were in the desert today listening to John, what dreams might come to mind for us? Would you like to see your marriage become stronger? Do we dream for a more peaceful world free from terrorism? Perhaps there is a broken relationship between ourselves and someone that we would like to see healed. Maybe things are OK for us, but just kind of ordinary—kind of bland. Do we dream of a more serious relationship with our Lord? John proclaims that all of this can happen in Christ.

Enter the desert. But before these dreams can start to be realized, we need to enter the desert. The people who heard John stepped away from their ordinary lives. They went out into the desert to hear him proclaim their need to turn to the Lord—to rely on Christ to let their dreams be realized. How do we enter the desert? As you are busy getting ready for

Christmas, as I am finishing the academic semester, do we have time to head off for a retreat? Probably not. But we do need to find ways to enter the desert at least long enough to listen to the Lord. Perhaps as we are wrapping Christmas presents, we might take a moment to pray for the person who will receive the gift. Maybe as we write Christmas cards, we could do the same thing—say a prayer for the people we are sending the card to. This Advent, I have found it helpful to take an extra few minutes sometime in the day to quietly be with the Lord. This is an added moment of prayer, just a reminder that this is a special season. We can enter the desert in small ways if we try. Advent is a time to listen.

How do I realize the dreams? Once we have met the Lord in those small desert ways, we have the power of the Lord in us to start bringing some of the visions and dreams into reality. Most of us cannot end terrorism all by ourselves, nor can we end world hunger. We can't fix the big dreams alone. But we can work in our own small corner of the world to help those dreams move along a bit further. At one end of the spectrum, Mother Theresa of Calcutta did it by founding a group of sisters who work worldwide to care for the homeless poor. At the other end of the spectrum, some try to make the world better by saying a few extra prayers. Somewhere between that grand program for the homeless and the simple prayers, we may find what the Lord is calling us to do. Someday, we won't need to put a fresh lamb in the lion's cage. They will get along just fine.

3rd Sunday of Advent, Year B

Sacred Heart Parish, Valley Park, Missouri

December 11, 2005

- **Season:** There is a great sense of joy as we eagerly anticipate the coming of Christ to the world.
- **Text:** The Holy Spirit calls Christians to rejoice and receive the gift of joy. As we respond to the example of John the Baptist to make our lives straight and to be witnesses to Christ, our real-world lives can reflect a particularly Christian joy.
- **Pastoral Context:** How can we be witnesses to Christ as we respond to those around us who are genuinely struggling or suffering from loneliness or sadness during this season?

John Q and Aunt Mary Father John Q. O'Connell was an Irish priest in my Vincentian community who was a real character. One day he said to me in a very serious voice, "We buried my Aunt Mary this afternoon." "John," I said, "I'm very sorry to hear that." "Oh, don't be sorry," he responded with a twinkle in his eye, "it was the only decent thing we could do; she was dead, you know." There is something in the psyche of some people that allows them to maintain deep-down happiness even when things are going very bad. They won't accept how they "should" feel.

Do I have to feel good at Christmas? How we "should" feel comes to mind because as Christmas approaches, many voices around us tell us we *should* feel good. Television commercials tell us we should be getting into the Christmas spirit and buy more merchandise. Music on the radio, Christmas TV specials, Christmas cards: they all say we should feel warm and joyful. It would be wonderful if that were the case for everyone. And I sincerely hope that it is for all of us who are here this morning. But it is probably an unrealistic hope. It is no secret that many people experience loneliness and even depression during the holidays. Nobody needs to add more guilt to those feelings by thinking they should feel better than they do.

The real joy of Christmas comes from the Spirit. That said, it is clear that our scriptures are calling us today to rejoice. The second reading has Paul telling us, "Rejoice always!" The first reading from the prophet Isaiah says, "I rejoice heartily in the Lord!" John, the Baptist in today's gospel, shouts out that it is time to make straight the way for the Lord's arrival! There is a lot of joy in this Word of God today. But the joy spoken of here is not the fleeting kind of good feeling that comes from hearing Christmas carols on the radio. This joy (point to book) comes when the Spirit of God dwells in our hearts. When the Lord is here, we can be truly joyful even if there are circumstances around us that cause us to feel sad or lonely. The joy proclaimed in these readings is not just a feeling; this is a relationship with the Lord that is true, deep-down joy.

What It Looks Like As I read these scriptures earlier, I asked myself, who do I know who shows this deep-down joy even when they may not be feeling all that happy? I recalled a conversation I had some time ago with a religious sister who is also a psychologist. I asked her, "Sister, what plans do you have for the Christmas holidays? Will you get a little rest?" She told me that she would be a bit busy with her other fulltime job. She is also working at a shelter for battered women. Their counselor quit, so my friend will have to fill in over the holidays. She won't be getting any rest at all. When I told her I was sorry to hear about all the extra work, she smiled and said, "Well, I really love these folks. What can I say?" That is what it looks like to have this kind of deep-down joy even when we might not feel all that happy.

John the prophet: Make the way straight. How do we get that kind of deep-down joy? How does this Spirit of God's joy get into our hearts? The Spirit of God certainly moved in a special way in John the Baptist. As we heard in the gospel today, John says, "I have come to make the way straight for his arrival." As we hear these words so close to Christmas, this gospel challenges us to ask, "What do I need to do to make the way straight for Jesus to enter my heart?" Unless those crooked ways are made straight, it is difficult for the joy to enter us. What are some of the crooked ways that need straightening out?

How do we make the way straight? I know for myself that I need to slow down during this busy season to take more time for prayer. This is a busy time of the year getting things ready for Christmas. I find myself hurrying to get Christmas cards in the mail and finishing up various projects so I can go home to visit some of my family. In this very holy season, I sometimes do not just stop and take time to be with the Lord in prayer. I also find myself getting a little impatient with some folks at this time of year—usually the people I spend the most time with day in and day out. Maybe you share some of these same crooked roads with me. Perhaps others who are here this morning have different crooked roads to make straight. Maybe some folks have not been generous enough in giving to the poor. Perhaps there is someone in our lives we need to make peace with. Grudges tend to hurt us much more than they do the person we have something against. This Advent is the time to ask the Lord to straighten out those crooked roads in our lives so that he has a clear path to our hearts.

We are witnesses, too—like John. John the Baptist goes beyond just telling us to make the road straight. He also says that he has come to be a witness to Jesus, who will follow after him. "I am not the light," John says. "Don't give me the glory. I am a witness to the light. I have come to point out Jesus, who is the true light." That, too, is a challenge for you and me. Like John the Baptist, you and I are called to witness to Jesus. People need to look at us and see that the Lord has made a difference in our lives.

There was an old rabbi who longed to see the arrival of the Messiah. As you know, our Jewish brothers and sisters do not believe the Lord has come. They still await the Messiah. This old rabbi prayed and longed to see that day. Each morning he would wake up and wonder if the savior had come. Each day, he would get out of bed, go to the window of his little shop, and look out on the street. And each day, he would see the same thing. He would see people pushing and shoving one another to get where they were going. He would see rudeness and scowling, unhappy faces. And each day, the rabbi would conclude the same thing, "No, no sign of the Messiah yet." He knew that when the Lord came, people would be at peace. People would be truly joyful. They would show this by the way they treated one another. This Christmas, if others are going to believe that Jesus truly has come, they will look at you and me and see if the Lord has made a difference to us. We, like John the Baptist, are to be witnesses. How might we show others that we believe Jesus is here? That would be worth thinking about in this time of Advent, wouldn't it?

The Eucharist We believe that the savior has come. We await his special coming into our hearts on Christmas day. Meanwhile, there are crooked ways to be made straight and witnessing to be done. That is why it is so important for us to be at this Eucharist. The Lord has come, and the Lord is here. As we receive the Lord at this table, we ask that he fill us with deep-down peace and joy. A peace and joy that is evident to others who see how we live.

4th Sunday of Advent, Year B

Sacred Heart Parish, Valley Park, Missouri

December 18, 2005

- **Season:** Christmas is a time of tradition in which we experience great wonder in contemplating the Incarnation and the value of human life.
- **Text:** In the first reading, we learn that the House of David was not a mere building but a house composed of people. In the Annunciation, that lineage comes to fulfillment in the boldness of Mary's yes to the angel.
- **Pastoral Context:** Our cultural and Christian heritage holds a special place in our lives. It is not a mere part of our history, but it is something that is lived and shared with those we love and encounter.

Family Heritage Sometimes, at Christmas and other holidays, my family has had as many as four generations gathered at our house. Those were good times to get out the family albums. I can still remember the first time I looked at pictures of my grandfathers who had died before I was born. Recently, I discovered the obituary for one of my grandfathers when I was going through my mother's papers. The obituary read, "Matthew Harris died this past Thursday. He was one of the most beloved men in town." I liked reading that. I had a sense of having a proud heritage. Heritage really matters—we want to know where we came from. We have several adopted people in our family who have gone on extensive searches to find their birth parents and siblings. Although they are happy to be in our family, they still want to know where they came from. Heritage is a central theme in our Scriptures today. God's Word speaks of where the human family has come from in the past and where it is going in the future.

Second Samuel—House of David King David, as we heard in the Book of Samuel, decided he should build a house for the Lord. He is thinking of a physical building, perhaps a temple. But God turns the tables on David. God says, "Listen, son. You were just a lowly shepherd boy when I chose you as a future king. I have always looked out for you. Don't be worrying about building me a house. When your ancestors wandered for forty years in the desert, did I need a house then?" In those years of desert wandering, Moses would set up a meeting tent on the first day of each month, and God's Spirit would descend upon that tent in a cloud. God was happy to travel along with his people without a building of stone. "I will build you a house," God says to David. Of course, God is not talking only about a building made of stone and wood. Yes, David's son Solomon would construct the mighty Jerusalem temple. But it is clear here that God promises to build a house composed of a people. God will be with his chosen people and will remain with this House of David. God's people will always have that proud heritage, that knowledge that they were specially chosen and especially loved.

Luke—Annunciation We heard in the gospel today where that promise to the House of David led. Mary is the wife of Joseph of the House of David. God has worked all through the centuries among his people, moving to this most profound moment of his love for us when he sends an angel to the house of the young Jewish virgin, Mary. In the ancient language, the name "Mary" means *excellence*. We heard how Gabriel greets this excellent one by calling her the highly favored daughter. God has been active in his people all through the generations until this highly favored woman would give birth to Jesus.

Mary's Question to the Angel A Protestant preacher I know was asked to write a poem about this Annunciation event. I was really struck by the way he began the poem. It starts, "Mary, you who had the courage to question the word of an angel . . . " That is rather startling when you think about it. Here is an archangel announcing the birth of the savior. And Mary asks, "But how can this be? I am a virgin." Her question allows the angel to tell her and us a very important thing about the birth of Jesus. God will send His Holy Spirit to overshadow Mary. Every good Jew would recognize that expression. They would remember that when their ancestors wandered in the desert on their way to the Promised Land, God descended upon their meeting tent in a cloud. God would be with them in their traveling through life once again. God did not need a house of brick and wood. God is all-powerful and can do anything. God will be with us in our daily travels through life.

The Old Stories Again This gospel is an old story that we have heard over and over. That is one of the magical things about this fast-approaching Christmas. Most of us enjoy repeating the old traditions. We don't need many new, surprising things this time of the year. I would suspect that many families bring out the same Christmas decorations each year. Maybe you decorate the house just the same way you did last year. Probably many of us watch the same Christmas programs on TV each year and bring out the same Christmas albums. Christmas is a time for such traditions. And it is fine to hear old stories over and over. It is also fine to hear these same scriptures again and once again to hear them with fresh ears. We can let the wonder sink in once again.

Wonder of the Incarnation It is a wondrous thing that God reached into our human history and became one of us. That is the story of these scriptures today. We don't want to hear one word of that story changed. If you are parents of small children, try telling them the story of the Three Bears. There is the father bear, and the mother bear, and the young baby bear named Irving. "Wait!" they'll shout. "There is no bear named Irving." They know the story—we are not allowed to change it. Believers know this story too. God chose to become a human. God chose to enter the world not among the rich and famous but to be born in the little town of Bethlehem. And God chose to make all of us his family. That is the story of who we are as God's people. And it is the story of what our lives mean. Even though advertisers at Christmas tell us that we will be much more valuable people if we give and get just the right Christmas gifts, God's Word tells us that we are valuable simply for who we are as his children.

What Mother Theresa Taught Us This was the message that Mother Theresa of Calcutta wanted so hard to teach us. She was a simple lady who had a major insight—that every human being was a child of God regardless of what they could achieve or how valuable they were in the world's eyes. She could especially see the face of the suffering Christ in the lives of the poor and dying. No wonder the church is cutting all kinds of corners to have her declared a saint. There are not too many people as special as she was. But the good news is that her life has inspired ordinary men and women to reach out to the poor in their own ways. I was talking with a lady a while back who told me how busy and stressful her job was. I was guessing that she was probably really looking forward to a nice relaxing weekend at home. But then her face lit up as she told me she was going to a shelter that night to work among the poor. She had caught some of this spirit that God is among his people and in his people. It is an old story, but one that continues to give us life.

Eucharist Christmas will be here in just a few days. May we, too, realize what a great gift God has given us in becoming one of us. We celebrate that gift with another wonderful gift. At this table, Jesus continues to give us himself. As we receive the Lord here, may we truly be grateful for the deep love the Lord has for us.

Christmas

O NE OF DAN'S MOST extraordinary skills as a preacher was his ability to guide his parishioners through understanding the gospel in light of the Old Testament. Aware that some parishioners may be less familiar with the proclamations of the coming of the Messiah, Dan was not afraid to speak about the prophets' prophecies and work. His bold preaching brought the faithful to an awareness that Christ's arrival to the world was announced from the time of the Old Testament.

Christ has entered the world to save us from our sins and bring new light into the faithful's lives, inspiring hope and love. God, of the Old and New Testament, is our Father who never ceases to provide us with the gifts that strengthen our resolve to be more faithful disciples. The following homilies inspire parishioners to see Christmas as a period of great thanksgiving for the gift of Christ and a time to bolster our faith with the help of Mary and holy family life.

The Nativity of the Lord, Christmas Day

St. Catherine Laboure Parish, St. Louis, Missouri

December 25, 2010, 10:30 AM

- **Season:** While gifts and family memories are a significant part of the Christmas season, we come together to celebrate God entering our world as a tiny infant to save us and bring us to eternal life.
- **Text:** Isaiah's prophecy has been fulfilled in our savior and redeemer, Jesus Christ. Our savior did not come triumphantly into the world, but he humbly came to a poor Jewish family that fully trusted God's will.

- **Pastoral Context:** How often do we consider Jesus as our savior? How can we allow Jesus to enter our lives this Christmas season and save us from the things that hold us back from God?

Old Enough to Appreciate Christmas This Advent that we finished last night taught me that I am finally old enough to appreciate Christmas. As a child, I was too young to appreciate Christmas. In those days, it was all about getting the toys. Now young folks, don't get the wrong idea. Toys are just fine—enjoy them. I'll be with my family later today and plan to get in a little toy time. But Christmas is not really about toys. When I grew out of childhood and was too old for toys, I thought Christmas was about getting really neat gifts. I remember well my first transistor radio, or my first audio tape recorder. These were wonders back then; a radio you did not have to plug in? Amazing. But that is not really Christmas either. Years later, I associated Christmas with family and parties with friends. And although that is a bit more noble than thinking about gifts, it is not really Christmas either. No, this past Advent, I realized there are too many things, even good ones, that cloud the real reason we celebrate Christmas. This morning, we have it right. We have come to this place to celebrate the wonder that God has come into our world as one of us. God has become a man. God has immersed himself in our human world.

What does it mean for the Lord to enter our world? What does it mean to us that Jesus has embraced our human world? First of all, it ought to be an experience of amazement. It is so amazing that God who created this world would become fully human. It is so amazing, in fact, that many people cannot accept it. Our faith history is permeated by two main groups of heresies: one that refuses to believe that the man Jesus is fully God and one that refuses to believe that Jesus Christ is truly human. The great news about the incarnation, God becoming one of us, is that we can always turn to a God who has been there—he has chosen to be one of us. There is a wonderful African American spiritual that says it well. "Nobody knows the trouble I've seen. Nobody knows but Jesus." What a wise insight. Jesus does know. Jesus has been there. Jesus is with us always.

Why We Need a Savior Our prayers and our scriptures proclaim that Jesus has come among us as a savior. I wonder if we reflect enough on why we need a savior in the first place? If we were to look over the self-help section of a book store, we would find there are all kinds of books that describe how we can make ourselves better persons. I went on the Amazon book site and entered the search term "self-help books." A few years ago, when I did this, it returned about 35,000 results. I searched self-help books again the other day, and it returned 125,000 results. And that does not include the videos and DVDs. We can do it. We can save ourselves, can't we? I am sure that many of these books, or at least some of them, have very helpful advice about making ourselves better people. And the Lord does expect us to use our gifts to make ourselves better people. But the bottom line and the real message of Christmas is this: We need a savior because we cannot save ourselves. I may have told you about something my spiritual director tells me almost every time we have a session. When I start talking to him about controlling my life, I can count on him to say, "God is God, and you are not. And thanks be to God that you are not." And just so I didn't miss the point, I saw a billboard on the way home from spiritual direction that said, "Trust the Lord." I think I get it, Lord. I need to turn to you more and trust you to be a savior.

Isaiah: Why the Messiah Is Good News Our first reading for this Christmas morning tells us that as a people, we have needed a savior from the beginning. That ancient first reading from the prophet Isaiah was written to a people who longed for a messiah, a savior to come into their midst. And they knew why they needed a savior. They had returned to their holy city of Jerusalem after years of being captive slaves in the foreign city of Babylon. Where was Babylon? Most likely, it was where modern-day Baghdad is located in Iraq. God's people had been through some difficult years. They needed God to set things right. This reading abounds with a note of excitement because the people see the hand of God starting to restore their lives. They saw the Lord coming to deliver his people. We are not victims of foreign invaders. But we still need a messiah in our lives just as much as our ancient ancestors in the faith. And our gospel tells us this evening that we have received a savior. Jesus is among us.

Gospel: Jesus Is Savior Matthew tells us that God did not enter our world in some spectacular, otherworldly way. God could have entered our world on a glowing cloud with all kinds of special effects. But listen to what God chose to do. He chose a simple Jewish girl as his mother and chose a carpenter as her husband and his foster father. Both Mary and Joseph had their moments of confusion over all of these angels making these amazing predictions. But they both also had a very profound trust in God. They both agreed to accept God's marvelous will. And God's Word to both was powerful. Even though Mary was conceived without sin, both she and Joseph certainly knew that their world needed a savior. Do we know that we need this Savior?

Words from the Pope Pope Benedict had something to say a while back about our need to accept this savior. He wrote that he believed there was a special reason that Jesus came among us as a poor, humble infant rather than as a powerful figure. As the pope put it, "Perhaps we would have surrendered more easily before power or wisdom, but God doesn't want our surrender. Rather, he makes an appeal to our hearts and our free will to accept his love freely, without coercion." And once we allow the Lord to be the savior, we can let go of trying to save ourselves. That is not easy for some of us. In fact, a physicist of all people, by the name of Bernard Bailey, put it this way, "When they finally discover the center of the universe, a lot of people will be disappointed to discover they are not it." But thanks be to God that we are not the center of the universe.

Silent Night There was a special Christmas moment that took place back in 1818 in the little Austrian Church of St. Nicholas. On Christmas Eve that year, the parish organist told the pastor that the aging church organ was broken and it could not be fixed by midnight services. "But I could play a guitar for music. Do you think that would be appropriate?" The pastor responded, "Yes, I think it would be OK to play a guitar this time." The pastor added, "And I wrote a little poem that perhaps I could read while you are playing." And so that night, in 1818, in St. Nicholas Church in Austria, the world heard in German for the first time, "Silent Night." We still sing it two hundred years later. It is such a simple little song. But it is also so noble. It captures well who Jesus the savior is for us. His presence that first Christmas went unnoticed by many, a simple birth, really. But what a difference his presence has made in our lives.

Eucharist Our scriptures told us of the power of the Word. In a few moments, at the Christmas Mass, I will utter some other very powerful words, "This is my body, and this is my blood." We come here grateful today that the Lord has chosen to be one of us.

A YEAR OF VINCENTIAN PREACHING BY DANIEL HARRIS, CM

Feast of the Holy Family of Jesus, Mary, and Joseph

St. Catherine Laboure Parish, St. Louis, Missouri

December 26, 2010, 7:30 AM

- **Season:** The Holy Family faced the challenges modern migrants experience in our society. While we see the Holy Family as a symbol of peace, remember that they shared the difficulties of real life.
- **Text:** In Jesus Christ, God's promises to the Old Testament leaders and prophets come to fulfillment. God never abandons his people.
- **Pastoral Context:** Our families are sacred spaces where we can encounter God in our spouses, children, siblings, and others. As we patiently bear the family burdens we experience with God's grace, our bishops invite us also to consider the needs of immigrants burdened by oppression.

Graham Green's Story When I was in a freshman English class back in college (this was way back just after they invented the English language), we read a short story by Graham Green. It was about the man whom Jesus had cured from blindness. Remember that passage where Jesus restores a man's sight, and at first, the cure is not total? The man says he can see people moving, but they look like trees. Then Jesus does a bit more, and full sight is restored. However, the author of the short story never mentions Jesus or the Bible—we just hear the story from the man's point of view during the cure. Well, all we Catholic students understood the story—we got the hidden clues. But on Monday morning, when we started analyzing the story in class, a Jewish student in class called out, "Why didn't somebody tell me what this was about? I didn't have a clue!" And of course, everyone went, "Oh yeah, he would not get this story since he had never read the gospel." Authors often do that. They leave things unsaid, knowing that their intended readers will get the point if they read carefully. That is what Matthew is doing in today's gospel. His original Jewish Christian readers, the original audience, will get it. They will know what this story is about.

Clues to the Jewish Christian Readers You and I need a little help in what we are seeing when we look at the Holy Family. They look more peaceful to us than they would to the original audience. I am sure most of us have stopped by the tranquil crib scene in the back of the church. I am sure that many of your families have been sure that your children have seen the child Jesus in the crib with the Holy Family kneeling and the animals watching it all. It is a peaceful scene. How many Christmas cards did we receive this year with that scene of peace on them? But the gospel takes on a very different tone today. The magi, the three kings, have gone home. And Joseph gets the word in a dream that the young child is in mortal danger. The evil king Herod heard the news from the magi that a new king was born. Of course, Herod misses the whole point and thinks they are talking about an earthly king who will threaten his rule. Since Herod cannot find the child Jesus, he orders the death of all young male children. The family must flee. The Jewish Christian readers will hear more than you and I hear. They will be reminded of the times that they as a people had to flee the oppression of evil earthly tyrants. Immediately they will see that the story of the Holy Family is their story.

Out of Egypt It is especially important that Joseph learns in a dream that he should take Mary and the child into Egypt. That allows the scriptures to say that Jesus the savior will come out of Egypt. Recall that God's people were once slaves in Egypt. Their lives were miserable. Then God raised up the great Moses, who led the people out of Egyptian slavery. And so our gospel today echoes the words of the prophet Hosea, "Out of Egypt I have called my son." You can just imagine all the Jewish Christians hearing this gospel for the first time saying, "Yes, yes, we understand. This Jesus is the fulfillment of all that God has promised our people over the centuries. This Jesus frees us to be the people of God."

The Poor Refugee And Matthew has one more thing he wants his listeners to hear. This time the message is not only for the ancient Israelites but very much for us in 2010. As Joseph leads his family from one country to another, as Joseph flees one oppressive ruler after another, we are to hear that God is with the poor refugee. God is with the marginalized. God stands with the immigrant who is forced to flee oppressive rulers. And that story goes on in our own day.

New Holy Card My friend, Father Jude Siciliano, writes about this feast, that this gospel calls us to replace the peaceful, tranquil holy cards with a new image of the Holy Family. Father Jude invites us to see the Holy Family here with anxiety on their faces. We see a Holy Family running in fear of their lives. It does not take too much imagination to see in the faces of Joseph and Mary the kind of scenes that we see all too often on the evening news. We have seen the faces of families in Iraq or Afghanistan, and even in our own country. We need to remember the faces of those poor left behind in New Orleans and the Gulf Coast during Hurricane Katrina. I was at a convention of ministers last year, and one of the preachers, an African American woman, said, "The country may be tired of hearing about the poor abandoned in New Orleans; they may want to put that behind us. But we are not going to forget. We are going to keep reminding the world how people were treated." For a long time, families involved in that disaster were scattered throughout the country, unable to return to their homes in Louisiana and Mississippi. The gospel reminds us that the story of the Holy Family in exile continues in modern times. This is not just a pious event buried in the past. God's poor continue to be forced from their homelands. And we cannot ignore that.

Our Bishops Right now, our economy has the headlines, and it should. It matters a great deal. But that means that some people are getting ignored; immigrants. Our United States bishops are trying to help us keep these folks in mind—not as politicians but as pastors. The bishops are talking about the plight of the immigrants basing their teaching on the most recent Catholic Catechism that teaches issues of justice. The bishops write that our current immigration system is broken—serious believers need to participate in political processes that will help fix it. In particular, the bishops talk about how many immigrants are taken advantage of by unscrupulous American employers. This used to be just a statistic to me until I started teaching at a seminary in California. One of the Mexican American students told me about his life when he first came to the United States. The only job he could get was as a migrant worker in the fields. It was so sad to hear how poorly he was treated. This is why the bishops call us to look at the moral issues involved. The Holy Family, as seen in today's gospel, are immigrants fleeing from oppression. We might not have noticed that before, but there it is.

Tensions in the Human Family But this feast of the Holy Family also reminds us that our human families are sacred places. We heard that beautiful reading from Sirach talking about how children need to care for their parents. We heard Paul tell us in the second reading what it takes to be a member not only of our human families but of the larger Christian family. Paul tells us how we need to ask the Lord to help us be people of compassion, gentleness, and patience. God does not wave a magic wand over us and turn us into these wonderful, loving people. As you and I well know, our family lives involve tension, disagreements, and misunderstanding. But real families rely on the Lord to get us through those tough times. Our human families need to be places where children learn to develop a deep respect for others in the family. And those life lessons learned within the Christian family, in turn, help children learn to have love and respect for God's wider family—even for folks of a different race or culture than us. May the feast of the Holy Family be a time when we ask the Lord to help us grow in love for God's whole family.

Solemnity of Mary, Mother of God

Sacred Heart Parish, Valley Park, Missouri

January 1, 2006

- **Season:** Mary is always there for us to be our support, our mother, and the mother of the church.
- **Text:** In the Old Testament, we hear God sharing his blessing and peace with the people. In the gospel from the New Testament, Mary takes God's plans for her life and quietly meditates upon these in her heart. As a child of God, Mary had the strength to question Gabriel and deeply contemplate God's will.
- **Pastoral Context:** As we celebrate the beginning of a new year, are we aware of the need to renew and strengthen our relationship with Mary, Our Mother?

Numbers' Blessing Did you begin the new year last night with a party? Maybe some will start this new year by making some type of New Year's resolution. We know it is a special time for beginning again. The first reading for this feast always contains this wonderful blessing from the Book of Numbers. God's Word on this New Year's Day says, "The Lord bless you and keep you! The Lord let his face shine upon you, and be gracious to you! The Lord look upon you kindly and give you peace!" A good blessing. And as we start 2006, may we indeed have God shine on us and give us peace. Of course, we are not just gathered here to celebrate a new year. Everybody all over the world celebrates the new year. But for believers, this feast day is also the celebration of Mary, the Mother of God.

A "quiet" Mary treasured all these things. I am sure that no woman has been depicted more frequently in great art than Mary has. We have thousands of statues and paintings in which artists try to capture this very special woman. And our scriptures also give us images today—word pictures. Today's gospel paints a Mary who is quiet and reflective. After this amazing virgin birth, after the little family fled from the cruel Herod who tried to kill the child, after so many mysteries and revelations, God's Word says today that Mary treasured all these things in her heart. She just held them here. I like that image. It is not a passive image where Mary just timidly accepts everything that comes her way without the slightest question. It is an image of a thoughtful woman who accepts a wondrous God even though she does not fully understand everything. Many people talk too much trying to explain God's ways—Mary treasures God's ways quietly. We could learn from her.

Mary Who Had the Strength But this Mary is no weakling, no shrinking violet. Elsewhere in scripture, we have another image of a young virgin who is told by an angel of God that she will conceive a child. Before she gave her acceptance, she had a question or two about this. She wanted to know how it could all come to pass. I mentioned a few Sundays ago about hearing a poem written by one of our Protestant brothers. This minister was very taken by that image of Mary at the Annunciation. I love this first line from his poem, "Oh Mary, you who had the courage to question the word of an angel..." It *does* take courage to question angels. But Mary had that strength. She is not a shrinking violet.

Mary the Intercessor A third image or verbal picture of Mary comes to us not from scripture as much as from our sacred tradition. And that is Mary as our advocate, our mother, the mother of the church. We are encouraged to come to her asking that she intercede for our needs with her son.

The Statue Story There is a story about a young boy who was told that if he really wanted something, he should ask Mary, the Mother of God, to get it for him. This boy really wanted a new bicycle for his birthday. So he very sincerely prayed to Mary for this special gift. His birthday came, and no new bicycle. "Well," he figured, "I will ask Mary to get this for me for Christmas. After all, Christmas is the birth of her son." So he again prayed very sincerely, but no bicycle. Finally, he got an idea. He took a statue of Jesus off the mantel and wrapped it in tissue paper. Then he wrapped that bundle in newspaper and put masking tape all around it. He put the bundle in a box and hid it way back in the closet. Then he knelt down to pray. "Dear Mary, if you ever want to see your son again... you will get me that bicycle." But of course, we do not need to strong-arm Mary. As Mother of God, she is our mother and wants what is best for us.

Galatians We can confidently call Mary our mother because God's Word in the letter to the Galatians today tells us that Christ has made us his brothers and sisters and, therefore, the adopted children of God. That word *adopted* is very important. When I was growing up, I learned that some children in my school had been adopted. As a young boy, I felt so very sorry for those children—what would it be like to discover that your parents are not your real parents? But then I learned that my best friend was adopted. He told me, "Dan, your parents had to take what they got when you were born. My parents picked me out—they chose me." I thought about that for a long time. It is a good description of what it means for us to be adopted sons and daughters of God. God, who created each of us, chose us as his family. Mary is pleased to be our mother. This feast that honors Mary really tells us how special we are in God's eyes.

God reveals to shepherds. Mary would not want all the attention on her today. She would want us to notice someone else at this scene in the gospel today. And that would be the shepherds who had come to see this newborn child. In all the Christmas paintings I have seen, shepherds are clean, dressed in nice robes, and standing respectfully by the manger. They look a bit like characters we would see in a play or an opera. The fact is that in this day and age, shepherds were at the bottom of the social ladder. They lived out in the fields tending the sheep—they were smelly and not very clean. If a shepherd walked into a cocktail party, you would hear a gasp and glasses dropping all over the room. "How did shepherds get in here? What are they doing in a nice place like this?" And yet, when God chose to be born as one of us, Jesus does not appear on CNN or the Oprah show. God is revealed first to shepherds. Mary would notice this. Mary would see that God says that he has come for all of us. Our dignity is not in our wealth or our power but in the fact that the Lord chooses us all. God has adopted all into his family, rich and poor, young and old, healthy and ill. There may have been just a handful of people at this first Christmas, but now all are welcome.

Eucharist We come to this table, not just as folks who happen to live in the same neighborhood, but as God's family. As we begin this new year, let us ask the Lord to help us get off on the right foot by making a special new year's resolution. To live more faithfully as God's adopted, chosen, sons and daughters.

The Epiphany of the Lord

St. Catherine Laboure Parish, St. Louis, Missouri

January 2, 2011, 10:30 AM

- **Season:** Today, the extraordinary event of Christ's birth is revealed. What was a seemingly hidden event is now made present to all people.
- **Text:** In the wise men, we see that they were open to trust in God and to experience Jesus as an infant. They did not see him as a mere baby, but they recognized he was the fulfillment of God's Word.
- **Pastoral Context:** We recognize that some of our fellow brothers and sisters experience darkness and sadness at this time of year. Following the wise men's example, we can offer our God-given gifts to those in our community who need our love and blessings.

Epiphany This feast of the Epiphany helped me look very intelligent one day when I was a student in a graduate English literature course. In that class, we were studying various elements of writing when the professor asked, "Who knows the meaning of the literary device called "epiphany?" Nobody had studied that part of the chapter, including me. That's when the professor looked at me and said, "I'm sure that Father Harris can tell us all what 'epiphany' means." For a moment, I panicked. If you are in school right now, you know that sinking feeling. Then I suddenly realized why she called on Father. It was because the feast of the Epiphany is the time when the once hidden birth of Jesus is made known to all the world. What was once hidden is now revealed. It is a moment of "Aha—now I see it." And I answered the professor very calmly, "Well, epiphany as a literary device means that what had been hidden is now revealed, shown forth to all"—and I said it as if, "Doesn't everyone know this?" Today you and I celebrate the day that the hidden secret about Jesus was made public.

The Aha of the Epiphany Jesus is shown in the gospel today as being a very ordinary child born in rather humble circumstances. This birth was not announced on the society page of the *Bethlehem Post-Dispatch*. And that is the point of this feast of the Epiphany. This obscure, this hidden birth is being made known to the nations. The three wise men had the wisdom to find the Lord in the ordinary. They were able to see an ancient promise where so many others missed the point.

We are let in on the promise to the Jews. Way back in the Book of Genesis, the very first book of our scriptures, we hear about a solemn promise. God promised Adam and Eve that someday, someone will come to defeat the wily serpent, Satan. As the Word of God develops through the centuries, we hear the promises made to Abraham and all his descendants. Clearly, God, for whatever reason, had chosen the Jewish people as his own special people. It is to them that he will first reveal the promise. What this feast of the Epiphany tells us is that we Gentiles are also let in on the promise made first only to the Jews. The wise men are led to the holy city of Jerusalem by the star. They are looking for the newborn king. They have their gifts of gold, frankincense, and myrrh with them. Pious Jews offered such sacrifices to their God in the Jerusalem temple. But the three wise men do not offer these gifts in the holy temple. Instead, the star leads them to Bethlehem and to the house where they found Jesus, Mary, and Joseph. Once they see and believe, *then* they offer their gifts. They do the Jewish custom of offering. When they are ready to go back home, God tells them in a dream to return a different way, not to return to evil king Herod. Recall that God had also spoken to Joseph in dreams several times. These are marvelous literary ways that God's Word tells us the three kings are brought into the secret. That God's promise is not just for the Jews, it is for all of us.

Paul says the secret is shared. Paul's Letter to the Ephesians today also says that the secret is out. God planned all along to send his son for all people. Only gradually did God reveal the mystery. Only gradually was there an epiphany so that all could get in on the great secret. It is a great experience to be let in on a wonderful secret, isn't it? In the seminary back in California where I used to teach, one of my jobs was to help faculty with their use of computer technology in teaching. Every now and then, I had to consult our real expert who actually knew what he was doing—the tech support person whom we paid. He would teach me the secrets. I just loved learning the computer secrets. The wizard likes to share the secrets too. The Lord is enjoying sharing this great secret with us today.

Feeling Out of It at Christmas (Isaiah—Clouds and Light) This feast can be especially good news for those folks who have felt out of it during the Christmas season. Let's face it, everybody smiles at Christmas, and everyone shouts out, "Merry Christmas," but inside, some people find this a painful time of the year. We won't go into all the reasons because if someone feels out of it, they usually know exactly why. It is a bit like living under a dark cloud. God's Word knows about that feeling. Did you notice that the first reading today from Isaiah talks about dark clouds? "Darkness covers the earth," the reading says. That phrase is meant to remind the believer of the creation of the world. Genesis says that "darkness covered the earth." All was a big void. This is an apt image for how many folks can feel at Christmas if they are in pain of one kind or another. But the Lord is the great light that has come to scatter that darkness. It's no accident that the three wise men followed a star to Bethlehem. That star, that light, reminds us that Jesus revealed is the light of the world who has come to scatter the darkness that is in our hearts. Maybe some of us might not feel the kind of joy at Christmas that Bing Crosby sings about, but we can experience the joy of knowing that the Lord is in our midst.

We express our faith with gifts. Once the three kings realized who the Lord was, they offered their gifts. Much has been written on the symbolism of gold, frankincense, and myrrh. But it is also important to remember it is the thought that counts. These are *gifts* that expressed the inner faith of the wise men. On this day, when we celebrate the Lord who is given to all people, we too are called to offer gifts. We don't bring gold, frankincense, and myrrh to the stable, but we give something of ourselves to express the gratitude that is inside of us. The Lord has given us his life; what do we give?

Contemporary Needs Many of you gave Christmas gifts to the poor during Advent. I am sure that many more have donated to special charities. Perhaps some of you have already given help to those affected by our tornado. There are many generous people in this parish and in this country. We understand that being part of God's family means giving of ourselves in very practical ways. The Lord continually calls us to share of ourselves as an expression of our faith. Giving from our material resources is just one way we emulate the three kings who were giving of themselves. There are many ways for us to give of ourselves. We can give our time to those who need it. Perhaps someone in our own home needs a bit more time and understanding than we have given them lately. Perhaps some of us need to give more of our time and attention to the Lord in prayer. Even if we have already taken down our Christmas trees at home, even if all the Christmas decorations and sales are gone from the stores, let us as believers remember that what truly matters about this great feast is never put away but becomes a permanent part of our lives.

Eucharist I have stood at a crib scene sometimes and said to myself, "Wouldn't it be great to have been at Bethlehem? Wouldn't it have been wonderful to travel along with the three kings to see what they saw?" But we don't need to do that. We have the Lord here at this Eucharist. We have the Lord who continues to give himself at this table. In the spirit of the Epiphany, let us open our hearts here to receive the great gift of Jesus. And let us, in turn, give of our hearts in whatever way the Lord is calling us.

The Feast of the Baptism of the Lord

St. Catherine Laboure Parish, St. Louis, Missouri

January 9, 2011, 9 AM

- **Season:** As the liturgical season of Christmas comes to a close, this feast invites disciples to bring the guiding light of this season into our daily lives of ordinary time.
- **Text:** In the first reading, we encounter the Israelites who are hopeless and suffering under the Babylonians. God does not abandon his people but promises to send a servant to rescue them.
- **Pastoral Context:** In our lives, there may come a time when we feel abandoned or separated from God. One of the most important things we can do to face this despair head-on is to have hope. Through our baptism, God has gifted us with graces and virtues to preserve and fortify our spirits in times of darkness.

Need For Deliverance For most of my life, I lived here in the Midwest with people just like me; middle-class white folks. But back when I lived at a seminary near Los Angeles, I received a real education in how diverse our world is. We had students from about twenty different countries. The flags of our countries remind us too how wide our world is. It was quite an education for me to hear the stories from some of these seminarians from all over the world. Vietnamese students talked about growing up under a Communist regime that put some members of their families in jail. Some talked about harrowing escapes in leaky boats—then the long months at refugee camps. Students from Central America talked about rebel soldiers invading their villages. And on and on. A lot of people throughout the world in our own time long for deliverance from injustice. Just imagine what it would be like to go to bed hungry or to wake up fearful that this might be the day you would be arrested without even being told why. And, of course, we so often see the pictures on the television news that show the suffering people in Iraq, Afghanistan, Haiti, and so many other places. If we let ourselves feel their discouragement, we can see why our first reading has such an important and hopeful message.

The people feel abandoned. God's people, the Israelites, were also in a bad spot; they needed deliverance. We have heard about that exile through much of the Advent and Christmas season in our scripture readings. The Israelites had been forcibly taken from their homeland and brought into exile in Babylon. It was a time when the foreign power of Babylon overthrew the chosen people, seized and destroyed the holy city of Jerusalem, and hauled many people off to exile. What was particularly sad for the Israelites was their sense that God somehow must have abandoned them. They certainly must have felt that they had fallen from their favored state. That is why today's reading from Isaiah is such good news for God's people. God's Word says that the Lord will send a servant, a gentle healer who will bring light to the people. God has not abandoned his own people. God is still their champion. A servant will come to rescue the people.

Our Need for Jesus Is this Word also good news for us living our relatively peaceful lives in 2011? It is good news if we, too, realize our need for the Lord to rescue us from our own exiles. You and I have not been taken into Babylon or taken into exile by a foreign government, but we have our own hurts. And that's the point of this Word for us. Some of us may feel stressed by our work or home life. Perhaps some of the younger folks may not be understood at school. Some may be facing serious illnesses. Whatever the challenges we face, God's Word tells us that our lives will never be complete unless we have the Lord as the center of our lives. That does not mean that everything will be peachy for us, but it does mean that is the purpose of our lives. Some people do not believe this. They find ways to fill up their lives with money, busyness, shallow relationships, or countless other strategies. But the bottom line is this: We were created to live in a relationship with the Lord, and until we open ourselves to the Lord, our lives will never be really full. That is why the reading from Isaiah is good news for us too. We, too, are promised a servant who will make sense of our lives.

Jesus fulfills the hope. Our gospel shows us that Jesus has come among us to fulfill that ancient promise given to a people who felt God had forgotten them. Many people who were seeking to make sense of their lives were coming to John the Baptist to receive baptism, a baptism of forgiveness and renewal. They felt their lives were somehow empty. Perhaps they had relied on too many phony religious leaders and could see that John, at last, was the real article. Jesus, too, comes for this baptism. But Jesus is baptized not because he needs to be forgiven for his sins—he never sinned. This public act allows the bystanders and us to hear who Jesus really is and what his mission is. The voice from the cloud, the voice of God, proclaims that "This is my beloved son. Listen to him." If we want our lives to make sense, if we want to live for the reason we were created, we need to listen to Jesus and be his followers.

Superior General and Chinese Priest What does it look like to be this kind of follower of Jesus? The previous Vincentian Superior General, the big boss of my religious community who lives in Rome, wrote about his experience of meeting a true disciple. He wrote about his visit to China to see the Vincentians working there. He told some moving stories about Vincentian priests who had to be in hiding for years and years because the Communist government would not let them exercise their ministry in any public way. He went to visit one of these very old priests; I think he was about ninety years old. The priest moved in at his sister's house, where he would celebrate Mass secretly. In fact, his entire ministry was done in secret. The Superior General was led by guides to the modest house where the old priest lived. The relative who owned the house needed to lock the old man inside when he left for work for the priest's own protection. When the Superior General and his guides arrived, they could see the old man lying on his bed saying his rosary, but they could not get into the locked house. The Superior General told his guides they had to figure a way to get inside. Someone found a screwdriver, and they removed the lock to get inside. The old priest kept saying through an interpreter, "Who am I that the Superior General would come to see me?" He said this over and over during the visit. But the Superior General wrote to us in his newsletter, "I kept thinking, 'Who am I to have the honor of being in the presence of such a holy person?'"

Our Vocation to Be Light for Others It is not just ancient Chinese priests who are called to be holy disciples of Jesus. As followers, right where we live day in and day out, you and I are also called. And we do not live in a country where we need to keep our faith a secret. In fact, the Lord asks each of us to let others know whom we have found. Can people tell by looking at us that we have found someone who has given our lives meaning? I am reminded of an incident I heard about a young man who walked into the local Catholic Church and told the pastor that he wanted to become a Catholic. A few days later, another man came with the same request. And a few days after that, a young woman walked into the parish asking to become a Catholic. As the pastor interviewed them, he discovered that they all worked in the same office downtown. And when he asked them why they wanted to become Catholic, they all had the same answer. They said that there was a young lady in their office who just exuded peace and joy. She did not go around preaching to people. She was just very much at peace. And the three new converts said, "We want what this woman has found."

Eucharist The liturgical season of Christmas ends today. The once-secret birth of Jesus is now made known to all. It is time to leave the Bethlehem manger scene and spread the word about the Jesus we have met. Not yelling on street corners—but by living our faith openly right where the Lord has placed us in life. We have a tradition on this feast of the Baptism of Jesus to renew our own baptismal promises. May we take these promises seriously and ask the Lord to help us live our faith openly.

Lent

Dan's astuteness as a preacher is highlighted during Lent as he walks through the desert with his parishioners to foster a proper understanding of sacrifice and fasting. Dan was keen to note that we as Catholics do not fast and pray for the mere sake of suffering, but we orient our Lenten sacrifices toward a higher good—God and his merciful love.

Having a pastor's heart, Dan knew that Lent could be difficult for those who struggled with their Lenten resolutions. Rather than rebuke or critique, Dan guided his parishioners toward two great sources of support and strength in the dryness of Lent: the Eucharist and the community. In the Eucharist, we are fortified by Christ's body and blood in our Christian desire for God's grace and peace. The Eucharist helps strengthen our resolve to grow as disciples of God and, in the context of Lent, discover where the Lord is challenging us to grow in greater faithfulness to him. For Dan, the community was not a nebulous term, but it is indeed the church and her members who are called to be brothers and sisters of Christ. Therefore, the community is challenged to turn to one's neighbor and accompany those who are struggling in the desert. When we are strong, we can help shoulder the crosses of those in our community who are burdened and struggling under the weight of sin and suffering.

Ash Wednesday

Sisters of Loretto, Nerinx Hall High School, St. Louis, Missouri

March 1, 2006

- **Season:** In today's readings, we get a bit of a juxtaposition in the images of fasting.

- **Text:** In Joel, we see that fasting is an act that is made public for all. Christ shifts our understanding of fasting from a public spectacle to a private encounter between God and self. Fasting should never be a self-serving act, but it should always be an act given to God.
- **Pastoral Context:** In the spirit of fasting and sacrifice, we should hunger for God and his goodness.

Playing Games with God An old rabbi was meditating on the vastness and the power of God. He burst out in prayer, asking, "Lord, what is time to you? What are 100,000 years in your eyes?" To his surprise, God answered, "In my eyes, 100,000 years is just a minute." The rabbi went further with his prayer. "Lord, all wealth is nothing in your eyes. What is $10 million in your eyes?" God again answered, "In my eyes, $10 million is just a penny." Then the rabbi asked, "Lord would you give me a penny?" And God answered, "In a minute." This is very typical of Jewish humor—our ancestors in the faith love to tell stories where people are at play with God. These scriptures seem to do that a bit for this Ash Wednesday.

Juxtaposing Images of Fasting The prophet Joel says, "Let's call for a big communal fast—let's make a big public deal of this. Jesus says in the gospel, "Don't let folks know you are fasting." Joel says, "Blow the trumpet at the fast." Jesus says, "When you fast, don't toot your own horn—keep it quiet." In other places of the gospel, Jesus says that we are to pray in common because when two or three are gathered in his name, there he is in their midst. Today he says, "Go to your room, shut your door, and pray in secret." Our notion of fasting and prayer is being played with a bit here.

Why Fast for Joel? And why is Joel calling for this big fast to begin with? It is because his people have suffered a plague of locusts and a terrible drought. They are at the bottom of their resources, at their wits' end. I moved here from California in July. We had lots of earthquakes and droughts and disasters. When those things happened, we called in FEMA and the state authorities. Joel looks at the disaster differently. He calls for a fast. He calls people to turn toward God. And as we heard in the pivotal last verse, God turns toward the people and removes their suffering.

Why Fast for Us? Jesus offers us a different reason to fast. There is nothing here in the gospel about fasting because we need to be relieved from some calamity. We are called to fast quietly and in secret because our fast is directed not toward getting attention from others. Our fast is directed toward the Lord. And here is where Jesus and Joel can shake hands and say they are in total agreement—fasting is about rending our hearts, not our garments. Fasting is not about what others will see but what God sees.

Hunger for the Lord Fasting makes me hungry. I wake up at midnight every Ash Wednesday morning really wanting a Krispy Kreme. I will be hungry all day. I may wake at midnight tonight, and if I do, I will not be hungry at all. But that is fine. Fasting is all about reminding us that we hunger. But not even the best hamburger and not even the best single malt scotch will ever satisfy that hunger. Lent reminds us that we must hunger for the Lord. Only when we feed here (the altar) are we really satisfied.

1st Sunday of Lent, Year B

Sacred Heart Parish, Valley Park, Missouri

March 5, 2006, 7 AM

- **Season:** When deciding what to offer up for Lent, we should remember why we are offering penance: so our new practices may bear fruit in our lives. Lent also calls us to recall our baptism and identity as God's children.
- **Text:** In the gospel, Jesus enters into the season of Lent by facing temptations from Satan. God has announced Jesus's identity, and his temptations all revolve around his identity as the Son of God. Jesus suffered pain from the temptation, even though he did not sin.
- **Pastoral Context:** Although we may face the same temptations many times in our lives, we are not alone in facing temptation. Our human nature naturally inclines us to do things our way, ignoring God's will for our lives. If we follow Christ and accept him in the Eucharist, he will strengthen our resolve to face temptation.

Lenten Games On National Public Radio this week, a priest was interviewed about the tradition of fasting during Lent. He began by talking about his college days before he entered the seminary. He was explaining to his two roommates why Catholics give something up during Lent. One of them was a non-Catholic, and the other was Jewish. One of his roommates said, "You should not be allowed to pick your own penance—you will go too easy on yourself. I will pick the penance for you because I know what you would really find difficult." This friend knew that this priest-to-be loved to drink orange soda all day long—it was a habit he developed to keep him alert during his study. So that was the penance. To this day, the priest said in the radio interview, his friend calls him a few days before Lent starts and gives him his penance. That might be a good idea for some people—to let someone who knows them well pick out a penance. But I like the way the church recommends—that we look at our lives and ask ourselves what Lenten practice might be most appropriate.

Meaning of Penance in Lent The church no longer gives us many specific rules for Lent. Except for the two days of fast and abstinence and the Fridays of Lent when we abstain from meat, we are asked to decide for ourselves how we will observe Lent. The three traditional Lenten practices are fasting (giving up something—and it does not need to be food), prayer, and giving alms to the poor. Each of us needs to choose some meaningful way for us to express the purpose of Lent. It is important for us to appreciate *why* we do penance so that the practices we choose can bear fruit in our lives. Lent is largely about baptism. In our own parish, and around the city and around the world, there are people in the RCIA program who are preparing for incorporation into our faith community. Some will be baptized at the Easter Vigil on Holy Saturday. We support them in our Lenten prayer. But all of us are also preparing for that Easter feast when we renew our own baptismal promises. Lent is a time to remember who we are as baptized people. It is a time to recall our identity as sons and daughters of God.

Meaning of Jesus's Temptations In the gospel for this first Sunday of Lent, we see Jesus going through his own personal Lent as he faces his temptations. He, too, had to deal with who he was as God's Son. This scene we heard takes place after Jesus was baptized. At Jesus's baptism, the Father proclaimed, "This is my beloved Son. Listen to him." The Father has announced the identity of this man Jesus. But Jesus's own temptations in the desert center around that identity. Mark does not describe those temptations—he simply says that Jesus was tempted during the forty days. But we do have the temptations described in Matthew. Two of those temptations do not seem all that unreasonable at first. Satan tempts Jesus to turn stones into bread (which he could do easily—and he was hungry). Then Satan tempts Jesus to jump off the top of the temple, and the angels would catch him. What's the harm in that? We know that Jesus is all-powerful, and he could do that if he wanted to. The harm is this. Those temptations are about Jesus's identity. God the Father has called Jesus to be obedient in facing his passion and death on the cross—that was the Father's plan for how we were to be saved. Jesus was therefore tempted to work flashy wonders, to take a shortcut around the path of suffering and death. He was being tempted to do it his way, not the Father's way.

Jesus was really tempted. It is important for us to realize that Jesus was truly tempted. He was not just going through an act here. It is true that Jesus did not sin, but that did not diminish the pain of being tempted. The gospel said that Jesus was forty days in the desert and was tempted during that time. It is possible, maybe even likely, that Jesus's temptations continued throughout his life—the same temptation to do it his way, not the Father's way. I suspect he was often tempted to follow his own will. Recall that powerful scene the night before he died when Jesus knelt in the garden and prayed that he would not have to face the cross. "Father, if it is possible, let this cup pass from me." And we read in the scriptures that Jesus's sweat was like drops of blood. And yet, in the end, as in his whole life, Jesus did the Father's will.

Temptation is a part of life. You and I are called to face this same temptation over and over—will I do things the way I want to do them, or will I follow God's way? We are not the first folks to face that temptation. From the very beginning of time, people have been tempted to turn away from following God's will and do it their way. Adam and Eve, in the first pages of the Bible, were tempted to eat the fruit from the forbidden tree. I think I once mentioned here that my friend, Father Charlie Miller, once observed that God should not have told Adam and Eve, "Don't eat the fruit from that one particular tree." God should have said, "Whatever you do, don't eat that serpent." They would have gobbled it right up. It has always been in our human nature to want to do things our way, not God's way. And so we people have struggled with the temptation to do it our way from the very start of human life. We are people who want to do it our way.

Remember who our God is and who we are. But the good news is that God has promised to be always with us in our life journey. He promises to strengthen us at times of temptation. That is the good news from our first reading today. The reading from the Book of Genesis tells us about Noah and the people of his time who kept wanting to follow their own will and not God's. Things got so bad that God told Noah to build the ark, load up the few good people remaining, and put in some animals because he would wipe things clean with the waters of a flood. The Lord is going to start over. As hard as it is to read about that decision from the Lord, this reading ends on such a positive note. The floodwaters receded, everybody had come out of the ark, and God said, I am going to enter into a sacred agreement with you, my people. We call it a covenant. And as a sign of our agreement, I will place the rainbow in the sky. Maybe that's why rainbows are so appealing to us.

Maybe something buried in the human psyche helps us recall our identity as people of the covenant. When a rainbow appears in the sky today, have you ever heard anyone say, "Oh, who cares about that? It's only a rainbow!" Most of us take a good long stare at it. We admire it. Next time you see one, remember that the Lord calls it the sign of his intimate covenant with us. That is who we are. That is our identity as God's family. This is what we recall in Lent.

Eucharist—Strength in Temptation In this Eucharist for the first Sunday of Lent, we hear this encouraging word from the Lord who strengthens us when we face our temptations to do things our way. And at this table, we enter the ongoing sacrifice where Jesus offers his obedience and himself to his Father. May we fully enter Lent so that we can more fully renew our baptism at Easter.

2nd Sunday of Lent, Year B

Sacred Heart Parish, Valley Park, Missouri

March 12, 2006

- **Season:** Entering the second week of Lent, we may realize that we are not living out our Lenten promises and sacrifices. With this in mind, we turn to Christ to be reenergized and guided in becoming better Christian disciples.
- **Text:** Jesus was a Jew who followed his faith closely and was a member of the Abrahamic covenant. In the Transfiguration scene, Jesus continues the mission given to the Old Testament prophets. The Transfiguration inspires us with great hope and encouragement because Christ reveals that his glory is greater than death and suffering.
- **Pastoral Context:** Our faith calls us to be hopeful in this life, even when we face trials and tribulations. We also hope to join him in the eternal life yet to come.

Jewish Parents and Love This past week, I heard a wonderful lecture from Dr. Amy-Jill Levine, the renowned Jewish scholar who teaches the New Testament—that is an amazing feat for a Jew to teach the Christian scriptures. She told us about growing up as the only Jewish child in an all-Catholic grammar school. Obviously, all of her friends were Catholic, and she liked what she knew about the church. She was a little girl when Pope John XXIII died. She saw his funeral on TV and was impressed with how many people poured out their love for him. She asked her mother who this man was that drew so much attention. Her very Jewish mother said, "That was Pope John—he was very good for Jews." John XXIII was responsible for calling the Catholics and all Christians to respect our Jewish heritage. Well, little Amy-Jill Levine decided at that point that she wanted to become the pope when she grew up. Her mother said, "You can't be the pope." "Why can't I," Amy asked. Her mother said, "Because you're not Italian, that's why." The point of Dr. Levin's wonderful talk was to help Christians appreciate our Jewish roots in the scriptures. And, of course, that Christians can appreciate Jesus better if we recall that he is Jewish. That is helpful for us to recall as we hear our scriptures today. The first reading recalls the Jewish tradition of sacrificing animals to the Lord. But this time, Abraham is asked to sacrifice his own son, Isaac.

Abraham's Test and Promise Can you imagine how Abraham felt when the Lord asked him to sacrifice his only son Isaac? One of the TV networks did a very fine film in which George C. Scott played Abraham. The scene that depicted this first reading was especially powerful. We viewers did not hear the voice of God speak to Abraham. We only saw the face of Abraham suddenly growing very confused when he somehow heard God's voice within him. And when Abraham got the Word to sacrifice his beloved Isaac, he covered his ears and pounded his fist on a huge boulder. He was absolutely devastated by this command. But as we heard, God was pleased with Abraham's faith. The life of his son was spared. And God enters a covenant, an agreement with Abraham and all his many descendants. We discover later that God would call these people his chosen people. God's beloved Jewish people enjoy a covenant with God that was not revoked. If we are to fully appreciate what today's gospel tells us about the Transfiguration, we need to see the Jewish Jesus as one of the people of the covenant promise made to Abraham.

Transfiguration—Mountaintop We know something special is about to happen because Jesus leads Peter, James, and John up a mountain. This is significant because, throughout salvation history, God usually gives his special revelations on a mountaintop. In our first reading today, God tells Abraham to sacrifice his son on a height that is an elevated area—probably a mountain. When Yahweh gave the ten commandments to Moses, it was on Mount Sinai. We know that as Jesus takes his disciples up the mountain in this gospel, something special is about to happen. And something special does happen. We hear God's Word proclaim that Jesus is seen in all his magnificent glory. It is very significant that the prophet Elijah is here and that Moses is here talking with Jesus. Jesus is carrying on their mission as spokesperson for the heavenly Father.

Transfiguration—the Encouraging Glimpse of Glory This gospel scene is a word of great encouragement to the disciples. They needed some encouragement just now because just before this glorious transfiguration, Jesus had predicted his own suffering and death. This must have been a cause for great confusion and discouragement to the disciples. In fact, we know that Peter tried to get Jesus to stop talking about all this suffering and death nonsense. Peter was either too afraid or too unbelieving to accept the Father's will that Jesus dies on the cross. And he certainly must have been downcast when he heard Jesus say, "Anyone who wishes to be my follower must take up his cross and join me." You mean we have to suffer too, Lord? But this glorious scene on the mountain today gives hope and encouragement. Jesus shows the disciples and us a glimpse of proof that all he has been saying is true. Although he will suffer and die, he will rise in glory. Death and suffering will be defeated. But this is not just about the glory that awaits Jesus in the kingdom.

The Kingdom—Remembering the Promise The Transfiguration shows us that we are called to join the Lord in the glory of eternal life. This is not news to any of us. Most of us have known since we were children that we are called to enter heaven after we die. But I wonder how often we reflect on that great destiny that lies before us. I will never forget presiding at one particular funeral several years ago. I was helping at another parish in the city where we were sometimes asked to do funerals at the local funeral home and not at the church. That usually means that the family is not particularly religious. I remember the unusually deep grief of one young girl in the family. The family had to gently pull her away from the casket, she was so out of control. It was as if she was feeling—"This is completely over. There is no more. Her grandfather is gone forever." But believers know something different because of the Transfiguration. Of course, we feel great sadness and loss when a loved one dies—that means we really love them. But believers know that this death is the beginning of new and eternal life. The Transfiguration gives us the hope and courage to face that day.

The Transfiguration changes the now. This transfiguration is not only about the ultimate hope of eternal life after we die. It is also about having a spirit of hope in the here and now. If we truly believe in eternal life, that belief will make all the difference in how we live here and now. That is what Paul is telling us in the second reading when he says that because God is with us who can be against us? Yes, we will face many trials and difficulties in this life. But the Lord is here with us. With support like that, what ultimately can harm us?

Eucharist The Eucharist we celebrate now is a promise of the kingdom. Jesus has told us very little about what eternal life is like, but he did speak of it often as a banquet. The banquet of his body and blood at this table is meant to join us with him in preparing for the eternal banquet. As we receive the Lord at this table, let us ask him to increase our faith in what lies ahead for us. And let us ask that this belief in the kingdom will help us know how we need to live our lives today.

3rd Sunday of Lent, Year A for Scrutinies

Sacred Heart Parish, Valley Park, Missouri

March 19, 2006, 8:30 AM

- **Season:** We ponder the sins that have become habits in our lives. Maybe this Lent can be a new opportunity to break away and get right with the Lord.
- **Text:** Jesus's living water gives us real life, and we can only find our source of this water, Christ himself. The woman leaves the well renewed with life-giving joy, and she feels inspired to share that joy and life with others.
- **Pastoral Context:** Have we been searching for our source of life-giving water? Or are we turning to other places to fill our needs and desires? Lent allows us to shed the things holding us back from God and enter into the life-giving water with Christ.

Thinking in a Whole New Way A few days ago, I was trying to make a computer program work correctly. I tried a procedure that I thought would work, but it failed. Undaunted, I tried the very same procedure, and again it failed. I kept trying this same process until I remembered that someone once said, "The definition of pathological behavior is to keep making the same mistake over and over." It was time to give up the old approach. It was time to try something very different. We can be like that in other areas of our lives too—not just computers. We can find ourselves doing the same unhelpful behaviors over and over. Maybe during Lent, as we look at our relationship with the Lord and others, we might realize there is a habit of sin in our lives that we have settled into—maybe it is time to break out, to take a fresh new look at our relationship with the Lord and others. That was certainly the case in this gospel today.

The Samaritan woman is changed. This Samaritan woman very likely came to the well as she did every other day thinking, I am sure that this will be just another day. "I need to go get the water," she thinks to herself. "I need to do all the same things I do each day." But then she met Jesus, who called her to question many things about herself and her life. And she was never the same again. Her world was different after meeting Jesus.

John's Four "Acts" The gospel story is actually a short play in four acts. As each act progresses, we see this woman gradually let down her defenses and come to see and believe in the tremendous love Jesus has for her.

Act 1 sets the scene that brings Jesus and this woman on stage together. It begins by saying that on his journey, Jesus *had* to pass through Samaria. Jesus did not *have* to pass through that area. It was not the only route. All devout Jews traveling in that area knew the kosher way to bypass Samaria. They walked around it. Jesus *had* to go through that area in the sense that he had an important mission there. He *had* to encounter this woman at the well. And the two characters, a Jewish man and a Samaritan woman, meet one another and begin to talk.

Act 2 of this drama is about a misunderstanding of terms. Jesus tells this woman he will give her *living water*. In the ancient language, the term *living water* could mean two different things. It could mean running fresh water, as opposed to stagnant water. Or it could mean *life-giving*, a meaning that was much more important. As Jesus and the woman talk, it is obvious that she is thinking of fresh water, and she wants to know where this water can be found—it will make her work so much easier. Jesus continues to talk about this great life-giving water until the woman finally asks, "Is this water you offer greater than what Jacob gave us?" Indeed it is much greater. It is water that gives real life.

In Act 3, Jesus begins to gradually call this woman to real faith. They talk about where true worship takes place. For the devout Jew, the temple is the only place of true worship. For the devout Samaritan, it must be on holy Mount Gerizim. But it becomes gradually clearer that something new is being announced. Jesus stands eye to eye with this woman. It is in him that she will find true faith. We can almost see her looking into the face of Jesus and starting to believe. We know from the longer version of this gospel that Jesus has certainly looked into her soul and told her all about her past life. But he did not do so in a scolding way but in the desire to call her to true faith. And she does believe.

In the final Act 4, the woman is so excited about her new faith that she leaves the bucket at the well—she does not need that other water. She has found life-giving water in Jesus. Her joy simply can't be kept inside. She must run to the village and tell others so that they too can believe. Once she has introduced others to Jesus, they believe, not because of her testimony, but because they too have looked into the face of Jesus. And so the play ends. But the story is not finished.

Where have you and I been looking? When you and I see a good play on the stage, we often leave as changed people. We want to take the values of that play back into our daily lives. What do we take with us from this play in today's gospel? Perhaps this gospel might challenge us to ask whether or not we have taken the time to look into the face of Jesus to find where real faith can be found. Maybe we have spent too much time looking elsewhere for what our lives are all about. Perhaps we have expected our job or our career to give our lives true meaning. Maybe we have thought that making money would give our lives real meaning. For others, we may have discovered during this Lent that there is some old habit or behavior that the Lord is calling us to leave behind. For others still, the Lord may be asking us to take on a new behavior. Do we need to be more generous with our time, our talent, or our treasure? Jesus is meeting us at our own wells and saying, "I love you as deeply as I love this Samaritan woman. Can I have your love back?" Lent is a good time for a change. Jesus invites us in this special season of Lent to look into his face. He invites us to re-discover that the real life-giving water is found only in him.

Eucharist There is no well of Jacob in this church today where we can meet Jesus. But we have something more important. We have the table where Jesus invites us to receive his body and blood. Here is life-giving water. May we leave this table eager to bring others to experience whom we have found here.

4th Sunday of Lent, Year A for Scrutinies

Sacred Heart Parish, Valley Park, Missouri

March 26, 2006, 8:30 AM

- **Season:** Jesus wants to illuminate our vision and help us move beyond our ignorance and blindness to one of great clarity and unity with him.
- **Text:** Jesus does not simply heal a blind person's infirmities. Jesus touches the man's spirit, and his eyes of faith are opened to believe in Christ. While some choose to remain spiritually blind, the blind man shows us that Christ is the way if we follow him and believe.
- **Pastoral Context:** Have we opened our eyes of faith to the needs of our faith community and those we meet in our daily lives? The Lord wants to expand our vision to help us be a light to those around us who are in darkness and pain.

Not Wanting to See Bad News A few weeks back, a news reporter for NBC television quoted a letter from a viewer who said he did not want to see any more reports about Hurricane Katrina. He said this story had been covered enough. Stop showing us the pictures; I do not want to see them anymore. About that same time, I heard a man interviewed on public radio who said one of his family members had died in the attack on the World Trade Center. He asked why the news had to stop showing the pictures of the falling towers.

I don't want to see it anymore. There is something about the act of seeing that really brings reality home to us. How often have we heard about some amazing thing, saying, "This, I have to see." As if it does not really exist until we can see it with our own eyes.

Jesus heals spiritual blindness. When the scriptures talk about real faith, about really coming to believe in the Lord, they often use the image of sight. To see is to believe. And to believe is to really see. Those without faith are described as being blind. Jesus encounters a blind man in today's gospel and heals him so that the man can now physically see. The physical healing is a great miracle, of course. But the Lord is doing far more than curing damaged retinas or corneas. An even greater miracle takes place. The blind man is now able to see and believe in Jesus. He comes to have the eyes of genuine faith. The sad irony is that some physically sighted people, the cynical people in the crowd, went away spiritually blind. They refused to see and believe in Jesus. The man once blind could now see; the physically sighted people became spiritually blind.

Not a Put Down of the Physically Blind The gospel stories use blindness as a symbol of spiritual blindness—refusal to believe. This is not meant to put down those who are physically blind. Some years ago, we had a seminarian studying at Kenrick from another diocese who was physically blind. I always looked forward to hearing him proclaim the scriptures. As he stood at the pulpit with his fingers running over his braille Bible, you knew he could really see. He not only saw with his sensitive fingers, but his voice resounded with the faith of spiritual sight. That is what Jesus did in the life of this blind man in the gospel.

Social Science Eye-Heart Zone The ancient people who first heard this gospel had a better sense of its meaning than we do. This was an ancient culture, and people think differently than we do today. In our culture, if we want people to understand something we are explaining, we say, "Think about it; use your head." Our modern science teaches us that the gray matter of the brain processes thoughts and allows us to grasp reality. But in this ancient culture of Jesus's time, if people wanted to be understood, they would say, "Look at it—see it." For them, the eyes were the way folks could understand and believe. That's why this miracle is so important. Jesus is saying, "I have opened your eyes so that you can now really see. You can now believe in me. You have the eyes of faith."

Scrutinies If you were at this 8:30 Mass last Sunday, you saw the first rite of scrutiny for the elect. The elect are those men and women throughout the church who are preparing for baptism and incorporation into the Catholic community at the Easter Vigil. Today is the Sunday for the second of those scrutinies. The term scrutiny means "to examine." Although our elect are not participating in the scrutiny at this Mass, many are doing so throughout the Archdiocese this morning. What they are doing can remind us about our own call to rededicate ourselves to a serious following of Jesus. The church is asking the elect to examine, to look carefully into their hearts, and root out all that does not lead them to walk in the ways of the Lord. The simple rite reflects very powerfully what this gospel is saying today. In the prayer of exorcism, the prayer to cast out all that is evil, the church prays that darkness and blindness will be removed. We pray that we may really see and may have real faith.

Our Spiritual Blind Spots Those of us who drive the highways each day know how important it is to check our blind spots. At least two times now, I have narrowly avoided very serious accidents when people drove right at me because I was in one of their blind spots. Blind spots can be deadly on the highway. But most of us have spiritual blind spots too. We have areas in our lives where the eyes of faith are not really open to see where the Lord is acting. Who of us can say that our eyes are fully open to the needs of people very close to us? Do we always have our eyes open enough to see others as children of God? How about some of the people we work with, or go to school with, or live under the same roof with us? The Lord wishes to touch those closed eyes of ours just as he opened the eyes of the man in the gospel today.

Lent: Let Jesus open our eyes. Lent is a good time for us to ask the Lord to open our eyes, to root out our blind spots. The Irish playwright George Bernard Shaw once said, "You see things, and you say 'Why?' But I dream things that never were, and I say 'Why not?'" President Kennedy was fond of quoting that line. It's a good Lenten motto because it can remind us to be people of vision. If the Lord really opens our eyes, there is no telling what we might see. When you come down to it, the vision Jesus calls us to have is not so much the ability to see the way things are. When Jesus opens our eyes, we are invited to see how things might be in our relationship with him and with our brothers and sisters.

Eucharist We need the open eyes of faith to be at this Eucharist. A non-believer would look in on us this morning and see only people kneeling before an altar with bread and wine. Jesus has given us the eyes to see this as his body and blood. Those eyes of faith keep us coming back here Sunday after Sunday. In coming to this table, let us ask the Lord also to help us have the eyes of faith to see his face in one another. Let us ask for the ability to see him in all those people and events of our daily lives.

5th Sunday of Lent, Year A for Scrutinies

Sacred Heart Parish, Valley Park, Missouri

April 2, 2006, 8:30 AM

- **Season:** Easter is coming soon. For this reason, we can have hope amid trial and tribulation. Do not be discouraged, for we will celebrate Christ's resurrection, which gives us power and strength.

- **Text:** In the reading from Ezekiel, God gives hope by breathing life back into his people. In the gospel, Christ raises Lazarus and brings him new life. Jesus's emotion at Lazarus's death shows us that God wants to breathe his life into us and lead us into heaven with him.
- **Pastoral Context:** In life, we will face many challenging circumstances such as illnesses, personal losses, and unexpected changes. These moments can be a source of great pain, but we pray and ask God to help us see how he is trying to breathe life into our suffering wounds.

Feeling Discouraged When I was a child (and mind you, this is a long time ago), there was a television cartoon character who was a laughing hyena. But this particular hyena never laughed; he was always looking on the dark side of a situation. He was sure that the worst would happen—a genuine pessimist. His name was Hardy Har Har—a great name for a hyena. He used to go around saying, "Oh dear, this is not going to go well. This is going to be a disaster." The cartoon was meant to entertain children, but I think of old Hardy Har Har when I meet some people. They never seem to feel positive about anything. All of us know what it's like to feel discouraged from time to time—that is a normal part of life. But some people face serious difficulties in their lives that leave them in a nearly perpetual state of discouragement. It is hard for them to find anything that brings them joy.

Ezekiel's People In our first reading, we see people like this—people who are deeply discouraged in their spirits. We see God's chosen people as very downcast because they are living in exile in a foreign country. Iraq is not only in our headlines these days but also in this reading. The foreign country that the Jews were taken to here is ancient Iraq, the area once called Babylon. The people were taken from the land that God himself brought them to. We can imagine them walking around with heads down, wondering if God still cared about them at all. Ezekiel, God's prophet, looked at them in this sorry state and wanted to give them new hope, but how could he do it?

The Vision While this spiritual death of his people was on his mind, Ezekiel wanders out onto an open field. It was probably a former battlefield because there were human bones strewn around. That is what God's people reminded him of—lifeless bones. And then Ezekiel has his vision. He sees God breathe the breath of life into these bones. He sees the bones start to join one another. And flesh begins to form on the bones and muscles. The bones come to life and begin to dance around. Perhaps you have heard the old African American spiritual, *Dem Bones, Dem Bones, dem Dry Bones?* That song comes from this vision of Ezekiel.

New Life The bones come to life because God breathed his breath of life into them. The Hebrew word for this breath of life is *ruah*. Way back in the Book of Genesis, when God took some of the earth to make the first man, God breathed the *ruah*, his breath of life, into that lifeless earth. So this is a prophecy of great hope—God gives life to his people. He brings them back from spiritual death.

Gospel Reason For Hope The vision of Ezekiel is echoed loudly in today's gospel story of Lazarus. We saw Jesus weeping at the tomb of his dead friend. When families choose this gospel for a funeral, I like to point out to them how encouraging it is to see Jesus weeping at the death of his friend. Jesus who promised eternal life to his followers could still feel great grief at his friend's grave. Tears are holy things that tell us how much we love someone. But the grief is not the main point of this gospel. The real point, of course, is that Jesus has power over death. Jesus has the power to call Lazarus forth—to breathe the breath of life into him and into all of us. For this gospel shows us that we are destined for eternal life. This is the reason we must never let ourselves be overcome by spiritual discouragement. Jesus is life.

Spiritual Discouragement And most of us do face many discouragements in our spiritual lives. Some of us may feel that our prayers never get answered. Doesn't God care about us? Some may be battling with various kinds of addictions that are controlling them. Some may be facing serious illness—or the illness of someone we love. These serious situations can leave us spiritually discouraged—we can feel a bit like Ezekiel's people—as if we were just dry bones. Lifeless. Sin can leave us feeling that way too.

Eucharist The message of Lent is that although we will at times face our crosses, and our discouragements, Easter is coming. Jesus who rose from the dead shows us that he is power over death—and all that can discourage us. He gives us himself now at this table. We enter his death and resurrection at this table. Let us bring him our discouragement, our crosses. But let us ask him to fill us with his breath of life that leaves us dancing with the joy of his deep love for us.

Final Scrutiny (Call up the elect and their sponsors.) Our elect will now receive this final rite of scrutiny. Recall that these scrutinies are times when those preparing for baptism and full membership in our church examine themselves before the Lord. Listen carefully to the prayers of the rite that remind us Jesus is Lord of the living, not of death. We pray that the Lord may root out all that is not of his life within us.

Palm Sunday of the Lord's Passion, Year B

Sacred Heart Parish, Valley Park, Missouri

April 9, 2006, noon

- **Season:** The people welcome Christ the King with palm branches to show him great honor and respect.
- **Text:** Our celebration brings us from a place of great joy to a place of sadness. Jesus is not a mere figure in the faith; he influences every aspect of life.
- **Pastoral Context:** Christ died for our sins, and we share in his death and resurrection. We must step into the drama and realize that Christ's acts in Holy Week changed our lives forever.

Outside the Homily: Most of us have probably been in a group that was honoring someone for their special service. We usually do that with a round of applause to show our appreciation for them. I have been to a few special events where the group really wanted to show strong love and gratitude for the person we were honoring. The applause was especially loud and went on a long time. It was clear that people were not just saying, "We are grateful for what you have done." The applause was saying, "We are grateful for who you are."

In Jesus's culture, people had a different way of showing their honor and respect. In their culture, they gave their approval by waving palm branches. So, if people are wondering why we are doing this ceremony, it is partially our way of entering the spirit of today's gospel. Like the people in Jerusalem, we rejoice in our Lord's arrival in our midst. Let us take that joyful spirit into our Palm Sunday liturgy.

After the Passion: Gospel of Judas Judas does not come off so well in this powerful account of the Lord's passion and death. He betrays Jesus to the Lord's enemies—we do not really know why he did that. When it is evident to him what he has done, Judas takes his own life. To this day, 2,000 years later, we use the term "Judas" to describe a traitor. Well, if you have watched the news this past week, you may have heard about the discovery of an ancient fourth-century text called the Gospel of Judas. Judas comes off as the special friend of Jesus in that version. The news has been reporting this as a great find. Does this change everything? What the news does not report is that there have been other versions of biblical-like books around for centuries. But long ago, our church, guided by the Holy Spirit, determined that our present Bible contains the inspired word. And in our inspired word as we heard it today, Judas is part of a most sad drama that leads to the death of Jesus.

Palm Branches A few moments ago, when we were outside, we heard a joyful reading, and we waved palm branches in a spirit of victory. But the joy has turned to a somber mood. We carried the palm branches because the palm branches that the people carried in Jesus's time were a symbol. They were not religious symbols; they were political symbols. Palm branches were waved to honor military and political leaders. The Jewish people of Jerusalem were protesting against the Roman occupation force that suppressed them. The people put great hope in this dynamic rabbi preacher Jesus to lead them into battle or at least to a political insurrection. How disappointed they would be by the end of the week—after seeing the events that we just heard in this powerful gospel. But how they would miss the point if they were disappointed. Because what just sounded like total defeat was a magnificent victory over sin and death.

Rembrandt We enter Holy Week today. This is a week for us not to just look back on what happened 2,000 years ago. This is a week for us to step into the drama that has changed our lives forever. A famous artist expressed well how our lives today are linked forever with what happened on that day of crucifixion. The great Dutch artist Rembrandt painted a famous picture of the crucifixion in which the bystanders wore the contemporary dress of the artist's era. Next to Jesus, the center of the painting, the most interesting person in the painting is the man in modern dress who is raising up the cross. That man is clearly Rembrandt himself. The artist was saying that we are all involved in the death and resurrection of Jesus. It is for our sins that he has died. That is the drama of Holy Week—how do we step into the drama? If you are able, please come here Holy Thursday, Good Friday, and Saturday night for the Easter Vigil. Come and enter the drama and the victory that has changed our lives forever. We come not just to remember the past but to meet the Lord who is alive and present in our midst now.

Easter

DAN LIVED AND BREATHED what it meant to preach the good news that Jesus Christ has indeed risen. As a pastor inspired by this hallelujah message, his Easter sermons often centered on encountering the living Christ. Christ is no longer dead in the tomb, but he truly wants to walk with us on the journey of life filled with moments of both joy and tribulation.

Dan helped his parishioners to see Easter as a time of great joy and opportunity for change. Christ wants to enter into the brokenness that holds us back from being fully alive with him. In the Eucharistic celebration, Christ feeds us and restores us to new life to confront the journey before us. Following Dan's example, we thank God as we celebrate the risen Christ who has come to liberate us from the shackles of sin and lead us to eternal life with him.

The Resurrection of the Lord, Mass of Easter Day

Sacred Heart Parish, Valley Park, Missouri

April 16, 2006

- **Season:** Easter Sunday gives us the tradition of renewing our baptismal promises, which helps us recall our identities as people in Christ and make Christ's life felt in our parish and local communities.
- **Text:** In the first reading, after the apostles encountered the risen Christ, they aspired to share what they received with everyone around them. The gospel passage challenges us to consider whether we can believe in Christ without seeing him. May we never tire of seeking out Christ in our lives, especially in the poor and neglected in our midst.
- **Pastoral Context:** Christ promised to always be with us, but do we genuinely believe that? In our liturgy, Jesus is making himself present

in the Eucharist and in the Word. We give thanks for his presence amongst us today.

No Jesus in the Gospel Did you notice who did *not* appear in the gospel today? Anybody? Right, Jesus did not appear in this gospel. We heard *about* him; we heard that Mary Magdalene found the empty tomb at dawn; she thought his body had been stolen, but we never did see Jesus. I did not have time to check this for sure, but I am rather sure this is the only gospel ever read in the liturgy where Jesus does not appear. Here we are all dressed up on Easter Sunday to honor the risen Jesus, and he doesn't show up. Or does Jesus show up in a way that we may not expect? Is he here, but we might not notice?

The Empty Tomb When the disciples Peter and John get the Word that Jesus's body is not in the tomb, they come running. But all that they see are a few burial cloths in the empty tomb. I don't know if Peter and John were good detectives, but you and I, the readers of this gospel, are asked to do a little detective work. If someone had stolen the body of Jesus, would they have removed and left the burial cloths behind? Wouldn't thieves just pick up a body and take it quickly away? Especially would they have neatly removed and folded up the face cloth and left it there? Thieves are not neat and tidy. Later in this gospel, the part that comes after this section we heard in our liturgy, the risen Jesus does appear to Mary in the garden. But this Easter Sunday section leaves us just with the empty tomb as if to tease us. As if to say, "Do you believe in Jesus even if you don't see him?

Jesus never appears to me. There is a touch of real life in this brief gospel. While it would be nice to be able to see Jesus personally—to have private visions whenever we wished—it does not happen that way in real life. A saint or two has had visions, but most of us are called to believe even when we cannot see and touch Jesus. We believe that Jesus has risen, but we might ask where is he? I enjoyed the closing scene in the old movie *Oh God* when George Burns played the part of God. Throughout the film, he appeared to the main character, Jerry, but now God was going to go away. Jerry says to him, "Well, could I just talk to you sometime if I need to? How will I find you?" God responds, "Talk to me anytime; I'll listen." Do we believe the Lord is always with us in that sense? He has told us in his Word that he is.

Christ Present in the Assembly There is another important way that the Lord is with us always, and that is here in the liturgy. We believe that Jesus is present in the bread and wine after it has been consecrated. But the

Second Vatican Council also tells us that Christ is present, in his Word, in the minister, and in the assembly. If we want to see the risen Lord, we have to do a little bit of looking. Years ago, our Archdiocese of St. Louis was hosting a huge liturgical conference. A friend of mine had the job of making a large auditorium suitable for celebrating the closing Eucharist. He was racking his brain, thinking of some way to make that room look like church until it dawned on him. There would be thousands of Catholics gathered in that auditorium for liturgy. What clearer sign of the church is there than the assembled people of God? Do we really believe that the Lord is present each Sunday as we gather here?

No Room in the Pews The congregation today is much larger than usual. Our churches are always very full on Christmas and Easter, and the few Sundays after September 11 when folks had many things to pray about. A priest from another parish told me about the lady who was very upset because the church was so crowded on Easter Sunday. In fact, she had to stand through the whole service. She was overheard grumbling, "Some of these people who come here every Sunday ought to stay home on Easter so we who come only a few times a year would have a place to sit!" If there is anyone here who is not a regular part of our assembly, know that you are very welcome, and we hope you will always feel welcome here. Christ is present in this assembly of believers.

What will keep them coming? About this time of the year, I hear at least a few people pray that those who return to the church this Easter will keep coming back. So I have been wondering, "What would keep someone coming to the church every Sunday?" If someone came to Mass just on Easter or a few times a year, what might happen during this Mass that would cause them to *want* to keep coming back? Peter, the first apostle, gives us an answer in our first reading today. He and the other apostles met the risen Christ, and that made all the difference. After that powerful experience of meeting Christ, the early followers became eyewitnesses on fire with inviting others into the church. So if we want our community to grow and be alive, people, especially strangers, need to find the risen Christ in our midst.

Being a Community of Welcome The early church grew from a handful of eyewitnesses into a worldwide body because the believers welcomed others. In fact, they went out and found people to bring into the church. So are we a welcoming place? Do people find Christ here? I believe we are pretty good at that. Before I started celebrating Mass here on Sundays a little over a year ago, I came to the parish for Sunday Mass without wearing my priest outfit. I sat over to the side so I could see what this community was like. And I liked this community. I wanted to come back. Sometimes I meet visitors after Mass who are visiting from other parishes or cities. They mention how much they liked being here. So do we welcome folks? I think it is obvious that we do. Can we be even more hospitable? We can try. At least in light of today's scriptures, we ought to gather here in a way that those who are looking for Christ will find him alive and well in our midst. This is what it means to live our baptism.

Renewal of Baptism On this Easter Sunday, we have the great tradition of renewing our baptismal promises. Last night, some entered our church fully for the first time by being baptized into Christ. As we renew our belief that we are a new people in Christ, may we ask to be people of welcome, so that all will find Christ alive in our assembly.

2nd Sunday of Easter, Year B

Sacred Heart Parish, Valley Park, Missouri

April 23, 2006

- **Season:** As the Octave of Easter draws to its close, the liturgy continues to invite our Easter faith.

- **Text:** In our gospel, Thomas lives the idea: seeing is believing. Christ challenges us to go beyond that practice by saying, "Blessed are those who believe even if they have not seen." When we allow faith to be our guide, our eyes become open to the true meaning of Christ's teachings and presence.

- **Pastoral Context:** The gospel today challenges us to put on the eyes of God and trust in Christ's words. We should see that we are not in control. Instead, God knows what will bring us true fulfillment and into fuller union with him.

Don't trust images. I have some treasured photos that I took of my mother just two months before she passed away a few years ago. What you can't tell by looking at her smile is that she had a front tooth missing at the time. It doesn't show because these are digital photos, and I simply went to the computer and painted in a nice white tooth. I told my brother about how clever I was because he took pictures that same day. He is somewhat new to computers, so I was surprised to hear him say, "Oh, of course. I added the missing tooth right away. Just painted one in." Many people now know how to touch up family photos on their home computers. In the professional world, film studios can create entire realities through digital images. The point is, in this digital age, seeing is not always believing. Not everything we can see is true. Sometimes things that look real are just ones and zeros on a memory chip.

Being Open to Possibilities Our gospel today tells us two things about seeing and believing. Thomas the apostle eventually believed only because he saw. But Jesus says, "Blessed are those who believe even if they have not seen." Thomas the apostle evidently believed that only seeing is believing. The other disciples told Thomas they had seen the risen Lord; Thomas would have none of that talk. "Don't bother me with speculation and dreams. Unless I touch the wounds myself, I will not believe it." We are familiar with the expression *doubting Thomas*. Maybe it ought to be "stubborn Thomas."

The Thomas Movie When I read this gospel for the Second Sunday of Easter, my mind goes back to an incident from my grade school days. I was in third grade when the whole school went to the gym to watch a movie about the life of Christ. I vividly remember the scene when Thomas and Jesus meet. After Thomas finally comes to believe that Jesus is raised and standing before him, Jesus solemnly says, "You believe Thomas because you have seen. Blessed are those who have not seen and yet believe." One little kid sitting about two rows behind me said in a loud stage whisper, "That's us. Jesus is talking about us." And indeed he is. Jesus has changed the old adage, Seeing is believing," into "Believing is seeing." You and I do not believe because we have seen; we see because we believe.

Inclusio Structure of John—Starts with Nathaniel This entire Gospel According to John is one long story about seeing as believing and believing as seeing. The very first chapter of this gospel tells us about Nathaniel and how he came to see and believe in Jesus. This section we heard today near the conclusion of the gospel is a story about seeing and believing. We hear that the name, "Thomas" means "Twin." Who was his twin? Perhaps it was Nathaniel, a literary twin from the first chapter. Nathaniel, too at first, refused to believe. The other disciples told him that they had found the Lord. But he was skeptical. Jesus came to Nathaniel and looked into his heart, seeing there the makings of a true disciple. Nathaniel finally believes. But Nathaniel is not the star of that first chapter. Jesus, of course, is the real focus. Jesus concludes the incident by solemnly declaring that Nathaniel and the others will see much greater things—"You will see the heavens open, and see angels of God ascending and descending on the Son of Man." Once the eyes of faith are open, a whole new world opens up.

Inclusio Ends With Thomas The faith encounter meeting between Nathaniel and Jesus from the first chapter is echoed again in this meeting between Thomas and Jesus near the end of the entire gospel. Thomas, like Nathaniel, is told about Jesus by the other disciples. Thomas, like Nathaniel, is skeptical. He did not just demand to *see* Jesus; he had to touch the wounds! But Thomas finally does see Jesus with his physical eyes and the eyes of faith. Thomas is not the focus of this gospel; Jesus is. As Jesus did after opening the eyes of Nathaniel, he goes on to make a solemn proclamation. Jesus says, "Blessed are those who have not seen yet still believe." The Gospel According to John begins and ends with people coming to see.

Our Struggles with Faith You and I are in a different place than Nathaniel, Thomas, and so many of the other people in the scriptures. They were meeting this Jewish preacher for the first time and had to come to see that Jesus truly was the Lord. We have already traveled that route. We grew up believing Jesus is Lord and God. Our eyes need to be opened on a different level. For most of us, this gospel story of Jesus and Thomas is a challenge to have our eyes opened so that we can see Jesus as Lord of our lives, day in and day out. It is so human to live as if we were in control of everything. But we are not.

My Messiah Complex In my own ministry as a priest, I have to have my eyes opened up again and again regarding who is really in charge of our lives. When I have talked with people who are grieving over the loss of a spouse or listening to people who seem to be facing hopeless situations, I usually want to have something inspiring to tell them. I want to do or say something that will make everything all right. But of course, I cannot give them that magic answer. I can only help them see that the Lord knows us in our struggles, and the Lord will bring victory to our pain. Human eyes cannot see this. Human eyes will never grasp what our lives are really all about. But Jesus has opened our eyes to see something very different. Whatever difficulties you and I deal with, Jesus asks that we let him open our eyes to see that he is with us in that journey. And he promises that our life's journey will end in victory.

Eucharist Our eyes need to be open to see what happens at this table. To those without real sight, we must look like a bunch of strange folks giving honor to little pieces of white bread and cups of wine. But the Lord gives us the eyes to see something beyond the signs. The Lord allows us to see that this is his body and blood. In coming to this table, may the Lord give us vision each day to see that he is with us in every aspect of our lives. Believing is seeing.

3rd Sunday of Easter, Year B

Sacred Heart Parish, Valley Park, Missouri

April 30, 2006

- **Season:** As we move further into the season of Easter, Jesus appears at various times to his disciples. What does this mean for us today?
- **Text:** In the gospel, the living Jesus has made himself present to the disciples. Because of Jesus's resurrection, each participates in God's family as Christ's children. We have been given dignity as children of God. In our second reading, John claims that everything has changed since Jesus's resurrection.
- **Pastoral Context:** How have we changed knowing Jesus has risen from the dead? We are to live out our belief in the resurrection by the way we treat others.

Loch Ness Monster One day, an atheist was in a fishing boat on a Scottish lake. He not only denied God, but he also went fishing on Sunday while everyone was at church—just to spite those foolish believers. All of a sudden, without any warning, the Loch Ness Monster rose up from under the water. The huge wave that followed hit the boat and threw the poor atheist up into the air. He was falling back down right toward the monster's open mouth. (This is pretty exciting so far, isn't it?) Just then, the atheist yelled out a quick prayer, "Dear God, save me!" Suddenly the scene froze. The man hung in midair, only a few feet above the gaping jaws of the monster. A voice from the clouds asked, "How is it that you ask me for help? Only a few minutes ago, you would have said that you don't believe in God." The man answered back, "Help me out here, God. Only a few minutes ago, I did not believe in the Loch Ness Monster either!" The story tells us a few things about faith. It reminds us that some people will not believe anything unless it is staring them right in the face.

Post-Resurrection Appearances Jesus does that very thing for his disciples in today's gospel. He is literally *in their face*, risen from the dead. You and I know the end of the gospel story—we grew up knowing that Jesus rose from the dead. But the first disciples had to come to believe what you and I have always believed. They had seen the tragedy of the cross. They saw their leader die the death of a common criminal. And yet, here is the risen Jesus in their midst. And just to prove that he is the real thing, he invites them to touch him, touch his wounds. "See that I am flesh and bones; I am not a ghost." Jesus even eats a little food. Yes, he is real. Yes, he is truly risen. As the church continues to celebrate Easter for several more weeks, the scriptures bring us stories of Jesus appearing to his disciples. We might well ask, what does it all mean for us now?

This changes everything. There was an ad campaign for a car company a few years ago that said, "This changes everything." The company had come out with some new design concept that they said would change driving forever. Their slogan really does capture the essence of Jesus's resurrection. The fact that Jesus has risen from the dead really does change everything for believers. The fact that Jesus rose from the dead changes the way believers look at the world. If Jesus is truly risen, then it means that each of us is truly his child—it means that each of us has a tremendous dignity.

Jesus risen is the power to face our sin. The second reading, from the letter of John, gives us further reason to appreciate what it means that Jesus has risen from the dead. John's community, 2,000 years ago, faced a serious problem. There was a splinter group that did not believe that Jesus was God. They did not believe they needed to have their sins forgiven by Jesus. In fact, they even denied they had sinned. They were doing fine on their own, thank you very much. Furthermore, they denied that they needed to follow Jesus's teaching that we love our neighbor. They had created a religious life in their own image—they wanted to take religion on their terms. In America, I suppose that we have the legal right to invent our own faith, but we certainly won't find the true God that way. The people John writes to here had created a religion without regard for what the risen Jesus was offering them. Jesus risen from the dead had changed everything, but these folks were not willing to listen to what Jesus was offering. One of the saddest parts of their disbelief was their insistence that they did not need to love one another. That is why John writes here so strongly that we who believe in the risen Jesus must *live* our faith, not just talk about it.

The Desert Wall—Sharing our Faith John's word here calls us to live and share our faith by the way we treat one another. His message reminds me of the story about two men wandering in the desert. They had been with a group of merchants who had become terribly lost in a sandstorm. These two were sent by the others to find help. After the two had wandered for days, they were dying of thirst and hunger. Suddenly, they saw the walls of a city off in the distance. It was no mirage. They crawled to the city with the little strength they had left. When they reached the walls of the city, they managed to crawl to the top of the wall and could hardly believe their eyes. Inside were wells of flowing water, all kinds of food in the marketplace. They were saved. One of the men leapt over the wall to safety. But the other man went back to the group so he could tell his friends about the city. That, of course, is what John writes about today. Our faith in the resurrected Jesus has to be lived. It is not enough to simply say Jesus risen "changes everything." If Jesus risen truly does change everything, then people should be able to see it in our lives. This does not mean that we all run around preaching to others at home and at work, or at school. But it should be evident in the practical ways that we treat others; we believe Jesus has risen.

ACA Appeal At this special time each year, the Church of St. Louis urges us to contribute what we can to the Annual Catholic Appeal. The donations are used to help those folks in our archdiocese who face homelessness. The program helps the unemployed, the sick, the elderly, the handicapped, and the unborn. You might find it interesting to look at our archdiocesan website to see some of the wonderful things that have happened as a result of your past generosity. I was surprised to read about Tony, an immigrant who came to our area from the California farm fields. He was helped out by the office of Hispanic ministry and is now at our seminary studying to be the first Hispanic priest to be ordained for our archdiocese. There are lots of stories there of real people who have been helped by you all because Jesus risen has changed everything. After communion, we will hear a few more words about this very concrete and down-to-earth way to put today's Easter gospel into practice.

Eucharist—Resurrection in Our Midst Jesus risen gives himself to us at this table today. Some young people in our parish recently made their first communions as they received Jesus for the very first time. They have come to believe at their very young age that Jesus is risen and lives among us—especially in this sacrament. As we witness their young faith, may we too be strengthened at this table to show the face of Jesus to others by the way we treat them.

4th Sunday of Easter, Year B

Sacred Heart Parish, Valley Park, Missouri

May 7, 2006, noon

- **Season:** The risen Jesus is the Good Shepherd who will never cease to seek out his sheep.
- **Text:** Jesus knows his sheep by name, and the sheep know his voice as the true shepherd. Each of us is specially made and known by God. In the first reading, Peter teaches the people that they should not live in ignorance and blindness but rather repent and enter into a fuller relationship with Christ, our loving shepherd.
- **Pastoral Context:** In the church, we must keep our shepherds (deacons, priests, bishops, etc.) in prayer and ask God to bless us with more vocations to the priesthood and religious life.

My Mother's Notebook I have many wonderful memories of my parents and how much they loved their children. My mother kept a little book of the cute things we kids said when we were very young. When my oldest brother was eight years old, he asked my aunt, "How fast can a snake run?" My aunt said that she thought a snake could go about twenty miles an hour if you clocked it. My brother then asked, "How fast would it go if you didn't clock it?" I guess he had an image that you would throw a clock at the snake to make it take off. You need to know that the cutest comments in the book were made by me, but I am too humble to quote myself. If you have small children around the house, write those great things down—you won't regret it many years from now.

Your Love for Your Children I often see how many of you parents who come here have your lives so wrapped up in your children. I wish you could see yourselves from up here during Mass—the way so many of you are enthralled by your children. Clearly, they are everything to you. Jesus knew that about our lives. He knew about how someone who loves deeply is fully involved in what is best for others. The image he uses to describe his own love for us, his people, is that of a shepherd. He is the good shepherd who cares for us, his sheep.

The Hebrew scriptures speak of God shepherding Israel. The image of sheep and shepherds permeates the scriptures. From the pages of the ancient Old Testament, it is clear that God wishes to be a shepherd for his people Israel. Moses and David were career shepherds when God called them to shepherd the chosen people. Later in scripture, Ezekiel, God's prophet, invoked this image in a more challenging way. Ezekiel criticizes the religious leaders of his time for their lack of true pastoral care. A shepherd is a pastor. These evil men were only concerned with shepherding themselves, not shepherding God's flock. But the Book of Ezekiel ends on a note of hope. God promises to send a good shepherd, one who will genuinely care for the sheep, shepherding them on the right path. As we hear in the gospel and other places, Jesus will be that shepherd.

The Shepherd knows our name. Jesus says something almost charming in this gospel. He says that unlike the hired shepherd who is only working for pay, he, the good shepherd, knows each of his sheep. Another translation says that he calls his sheep by name and his sheep know the voice of the true shepherd. Shepherds in those days, at least good shepherds, gave pet names to their sheep. Perhaps the name would reflect that sheep's particular color, so the name would be "snowball." Or the pet name might reflect its mannerisms; another sheep might be called "jumpy." Whatever the nickname, each sheep was unique; each had a name. The gospel writer takes great care to talk about how Jesus named his disciples. Not only did he call them by name, he even changed the name of at least one of them, Peter. "You are rock—that's what I shall name you." In the Lord, each of us has a name. Each of us is somebody.

The Shepherd cared for us. A priest friend of mine writes about the time he was with a group of farmers who were sharing their reflections on this gospel. One of the modern-day shepherds asked this question of the group. "If you have one hundred sheep and one of them jumps over the fence, how many will you have left in the pen?" Nobody in the group was going to get suckered into the obvious answer, so they all asked him, "How many?" The shepherd said, "There will be no sheep in the pen because sheep are so stupid that if one jumps over the fence, the rest of them will follow him." It makes me feel a bit uneasy to hear Jesus calling me a sheep today. Of course, I have to admit that I have made plenty of dumb mistakes in my life while trying to be a follower of Jesus. And it is very good to know that when I have made dumb mistakes, I have a shepherd who does not give up on me. Jesus is that kind of shepherd. Do we let him be that kind of shepherd for us?

Acts: Peter's Reflection at Pentecost Our first reading from this liturgy shows us what it looks like when someone has fully accepted Jesus as the true shepherd. We heard Peter's bold Pentecost proclamation after he had healed a crippled man in the power of Jesus's name. In the strength of the Holy Spirit, Peter stands up and explains to the people that in their blindness, they have crucified the Lord's anointed. Jesus was truly the one through whom we have real life. Finally, their eyes are opened, and they realize what they have done. They ask, "What must we do?" Peter tells them to repent and be baptized in Jesus. Don't look for salvation anywhere else. Turn your lives over to the Lord. Let him be your shepherd.

How We All Shepherd Have you seen Jesus walking around our world lately in his shepherd clothes? I haven't. Jesus is certainly here among us, but he asks us to do the hands-on shepherding today. Jesus shepherds people's lives through our ministry. Many people here in this parish act as shepherds. Some bring Eucharist to the sick and shut-ins, others lend their time and talent to work in the religious education program, others work in the RCIA, some shepherd us in our worship through music, reading, and serving, and on and on. It is so dangerous to name all the ways people do shepherding in this parish because we will forget someone—but at least you know you do what you do because it is a share in the work of the good shepherd.

Vocation Sunday This Sunday, Good Shepherd Sunday, is also the day when our Holy Father asks that we pray in a special way for more religious vocations. We began by speaking of the cute things children say. One of my nieces, now an adult with her own child, was at Mass with her family when she was just a little four-year-old. The bishop was visiting the parish that Sunday, and he processed in with his miter and holding his crosier, which is supposed to resemble a shepherd's crook. Just as the entrance song stopped, and before the bishop could say anything, my little niece yelled out, "Look mom, it's a shepherd!" The bishop was very pleased that the child figured it out. Modern-day bishops and priests and religious men and women have the role of continuing the shepherding. Let us join the worldwide church today in asking that the Lord send us the shepherds that we need.

EASTER

5th Sunday of Easter, Year B

Mother's Day

Sacred Heart Parish, Valley Park, Missouri

May 14, 2006, 7 AM

- **Season:** On Mother's Day, we thank God for those who were our first teachers of the faith.
- **Text:** Jesus, the true vine, gives us the life and joy that sustains our journey. Our faith is not just a mere set of words; it is a lived experience we share with God and others. In the first reading, St. Paul shares that Christ's gift of love and grace has supported him through times of great suffering and pain.
- **Pastoral Context:** If we, the branches, are not attached to Christ, we will wither and die. We must find our fulfillment in God, the true vine who fills us with all we need to grow in holiness.

Charles Ssebulime's Grandmother When I taught at a seminary in California a few years ago, I had many students from different cultures and countries. I encouraged them to tell stories from their homeland when they practiced their homilies. One of my favorite stories was from a young seminarian who was from Africa. He told us about the time when he was a young boy growing up in his village. He was fascinated with all the technical things in his grandmother's house. He enjoyed examining things like her camera and her radio. But he was a curious young man, and he used to take these things apart. The problem was that he could not put them back together. And that was his cue to run away real fast—he knew she was an old lady and could not catch him. But his wise grandmother did not go looking for him, nor did she send out others after him. She knew that sooner or later, he would get hungry and come back to her. He needed food, and she was the only one he could receive it from. He said, "That memory helps me to see what the Lord is talking about in the scriptures when he says that he is the vine, we are the branches. He is the source of our very life, and without him we cannot live."

Jesus the True Vine Jesus calls himself the *true* vine, and we are the branches. If we are to have real life, it will only come when we join ourselves closely to him—as close as branches are to a vine. Without the vine, the branches wither and die. Without being attached to our Lord, our lives would become very empty. We will not find the meaning of our lives looking anywhere else other than in the Lord, the true vine. This image of the true vine is part of a larger preaching that Jesus gives where he talks about his identity. He is not just saying, "These are the things I perform," he is saying, "This is who I am. Will you join me?" "I am the good shepherd" (as we heard last Sunday); "I am the sheep gate where my sheep may enter safely; I am the true vine. Will you root your life fully in me?"

Context of the Gospel There is a good reason why Jesus stressed his identity by calling himself the *true* vine. Earlier in this gospel, Jesus had been dealing with false religious leaders. Jesus had cured a man born blind. Some of the religious leaders, instead of marveling at this miracle, became incensed at Jesus. They had their eyes of faith closed—they were the real blind guides. Jesus warned the people not to follow these blind guides. Instead, they should follow him, the true vine. I find myself losing patience with those blind guides until I realize that I have my own false gods—places where I look for meaning. Most of us do that if we are honest. I'll admit my own tendency is to find meaning by working—sometimes, I put too much time into what I can accomplish rather than realize it is the Lord that gives my life meaning. Other folks might try to find the meaning of lives in acquiring wealth or power over others, or they look for meaning in various chemical dependencies. There are lots of ways to look for fulfillment outside of the Lord.

Family Values Dying? When we look for fulfillment outside the Lord, we become disconnected from the true vine. A while back, I heard about a disturbing trend in how some people are becoming decreasingly disconnected. A study from a few years back mentioned that men and women are spending more and more time at work. That is no surprise to anyone. However, the study reported that 62 percent of the people interviewed were OK with those extra hours at work. In fact, 28 percent said they would like more time at work. The study concluded that way too many people are escaping from tensions at home and seeking refuge at work. Work is becoming home. These folks are becoming disconnected from their families by choice. That is just one symptom of how all of us can find our false gods in other places. The Lord calls us to find him in one another, as well as in our worship. Jesus says, stay connected to me, the true vine.

First John—Live Love Our second reading today reminds all of us that this rich relationship we have with Jesus needs to be expressed in the way we actually live, not just by what we say without words. John, who wrote that reading, was facing a particular problem in his local church. There was a group of people who were creating a big problem in John's new Christian community. They were people who did not fully accept Jesus Christ. They did not consider him to be God. They relied on their own knowledge to get them through life. Most of all, they did not believe they were obligated to love one another as Jesus teaches since they did not consider him to be God. So John is writing to them to help them see the real picture of who Jesus is and who we are. He is trying to help them connect the dots. John says, we who are in Jesus must not just talk about love; we have to actually live it. Faith involves far more than a set of beliefs. Faith is a relationship with Jesus and with our brothers and sisters. No more than a branch could live if it came off the vine, we cannot be who we are called to be if we are not grafted to Jesus.

Paul's Reliance on Jesus We heard in our first reading about how powerful Jesus acted in the life of St. Paul. Recall that it was not that long before this reading was written that Paul was persecuting the new Christians. That was all before Jesus stepped into his life and spun him completely around. Once Paul (the wayward branch) became grafted onto the vine of Jesus, Paul realized who he really was. He also learned really quickly that he would need to keep close to the Lord if he was going to really be who he was called to be. Paul knew a great deal about ethical living. He said that he knew how he was supposed to live as a disciple, but sometimes he just failed to live the way he knew he should. Paul wrote of how he begged God to remove that mysterious thorn from his side. We never learn what was bothering Paul, but it must have been a difficult trial of some kind. What we do know is that God called him to a radical trust in the power of God. "My grace is enough for you," the Lord told Paul. Because God promises that his grace is enough, this is not to say that we have no more need of medical doctors or therapists by praying away our problems. The Lord works through the skill and wisdom of these professionals. We need them both. But all the skilled professionals in the world can't help us be fully alive. That comes from the vine—Jesus.

Mother's Day We honor today those special women who had played an important part in helping us learn about the deep love God has for us. On this Mother's Day, we honor the ones who were probably the first preachers in our lives—I know I learned about the Lord from my mother before going to church. In fact, my mother once told me that I misbehaved in church so much that she stopped taking me until I got older. God has a sense of humor. We thank God for those wonderful women he has put into our lives and for all the people through whom he helps us to know that our real life is in him. Let us hold them in our hearts as we come to this table to receive him in this Eucharist.

6th Sunday of Easter, Year B

Sacred Heart Parish, Valley Park, Missouri

May 21, 2006, 8:30 AM

- **Season:** Late in the Easter season, we hear Jesus say farewell. Yet, he never leaves; he remains.
- **Text:** Jesus's call to love is not superficial and empty but inspired by God's love and grace. Christ is the one who works in us to inspire our love for others.
- **Pastoral Context:** Are we living our love out and practicing it with others? One of the most significant places to encounter God's love is in the sacraments, especially in our Eucharistic celebration.

The Meaning of Love I really love working on computers. I love springtime when it is warm enough for a nice walk but not too hot and humid as it will be soon. I love a good night's sleep. When my parents were alive, I loved them dearly. I hope you have a deep love for your spouse, or your children, or your parents. I wonder if you join me in loving chocolate. Are you getting the point here? We use that word *love* to cover a huge range of emotions, from the very silly to the very important and lofty. Even when we use the word *love* to refer to loving God and God's people, folks use that term in different ways.

Jesus calls us to live love, not just talk it. When I hear scriptures like today's that talk about love, I remember how annoying it can be to hear people talking about love *in general*, not love in real-life, down-to-earth terms. Philosophers and even theologians can present well-intentioned, learned discourses on love in beautiful terms. When I hear these lovely talks, I sometimes ask myself, "But do these people really live love, or do they just talk about it?" These scriptures, of course, are not about love in the abstract or the general. When Jesus calls us today to live on in his love, he is talking about something very specific and down to earth. Jesus is talking about living love, practicing it.

Easter Message Shifts to Farewell This gospel is a most important Easter message. The shopping malls have long forgotten Easter and are now putting out summer merchandise. But our liturgy keeps Easter before us a little while longer. One time right after Easter I was walking past a store with a big sign on the door that blared out, "Easter 75% Off." I thought, "Yes, but for believers, Easter is 100 percent *on*." Although we are in the Easter season, as we near the end of this Easter season, our scriptures have changed in tone. On the Sundays earlier in the Easter season, we heard about Jesus rising from the dead and appearing to his followers. These later gospels have Jesus saying farewell to his followers; he is about to leave them. Next Sunday, we celebrate the Ascension when Jesus returns to his Father. Jesus is telling us how to carry on after he leaves.

Jesus is going but never leaves. The thing is, Jesus has never really left us. Although this gospel shows him sitting with his disciples at the Last Supper, saying he is about to leave them, he also does something that allows him to remain with them and us always. Jesus leaves us himself in the Eucharist. He is leaving but never leaves. This farewell discourse at the Last Supper reminds me of something Abraham Lincoln said about God. When Abraham Lincoln was elected president, he gave a brief but moving farewell address when he left his beloved Springfield home to move to Washington in February of 1861. That eloquent farewell reads more like a homily than the speech of a politician. He tells the people that with all the challenges that are ahead for him, he will put his trust in the Lord, "who can go with me and remain with you." That really captures the spirit of Jesus's own farewell to his disciples. He is going back to the Father, but remaining with us. "Live on in my Love," Jesus says. I am here loving you at all times.

Images of Love in the Concrete So what does this kind of love look like? We see the Lord's love lived out in down-to-earth ways all the time if we are looking. God's love is expressed when parents sit up all night with a sick child, when someone cares patiently for an elderly spouse, when some young person takes the risk of talking to the kid at school whom nobody else wants to talk to. But I remember one very specific instance when I believe that I saw God's love most profoundly. I may have told you about this, I am not sure. I was changing planes in Dallas Fort Worth Airport on my way to yet another meeting that I did not want to attend. I wanted to stay home. Just when I was feeling good and sorry for myself, I noticed a small boy and his mother waiting for a plane. The child was perhaps seven years old. Whatever disease he had caused him to constantly shake all over. He was in a special wheelchair with restraints. He seemed very upset—perhaps because of flying. And his mother showed me the face of God's love. She was just so relaxed and patient. She hugged her son and just told him that all would be OK. I was so moved by that sight that I wrote it down in detail. Sometimes, when I start feeling sorry for myself, I take that note out and relive that experience a bit. It keeps things in perspective, for one thing. But it also helps me appreciate something of what Jesus is saying in this gospel. "I am with you always; I am here. Now, my disciples, show my love to others."

Agape—Not the Love of Good Friends When we hear Jesus command us to love one another, we might wonder how someone can *command* love. We either love others, or we don't, right? When films and television and novels talk about love, they usually refer to the kind of love that is all about romantic feelings. Even when we are talking about love at its best, the special love of very good friends, we are not necessarily dealing with what Jesus is asking here. Jesus uses the word *agape* to talk about love. *Agape* is not about having good feelings toward others. *Agape* is love that is fueled by God's grace—God's power working in us. This is the kind of love that Mother Theresa talked about when she said that she could be joyful working among poor, diseased, dying people. When she saw them, she saw the face of Christ. We don't develop *agape* by our own efforts. It is the love of Christ in us that moves us to love others in this way. Our second reading from the Letter of John said it well when it calls us to realize that God *is* love. Therefore we must love one another. This kind of love that does not rely on feelings is an experience of God.

Acts: The Spirit is among us. This love that Jesus is talking about in the scriptures is also experienced at this Eucharist that we are celebrating. The Lord is here every bit as truly as he was in those ancient days of the scriptures. Maybe it sounded like ancient history when our first reading from the Acts of the Apostles talked about Peter and the early disciples becoming very excited to see the Spirit of God at work in the early church. But this goes on and on in our own time. The Lord continues to enter our lives in the sacraments. This presence is every bit as real as what we heard in the scriptures today. That is our faith. Let us come to this table today with the joy of knowing that Jesus who loves us so deeply is our food. In receiving him, may we live on in his love and share that love with others.

EASTER

Solemnity of the Ascension of the Lord

Memorial Day Weekend
Sacred Heart Parish, Valley Park, Missouri
May 28, 2006, 10:15 AM

- **Season:** Ascension Sunday invites us to consider how, in our day-to-day lives, we are meant to participate in God's mission in the world.
- **Text:** Jesus shifts the role of a teacher onto his students. Their mission is to bring to others what they have learned under the great teacher for three years. In Jesus's Ascension, he makes himself eternally present to all people, even in the trying and challenging times. Jesus is the source of strength and power for all believers.
- **Pastoral Context:** We must be a mission-centered people. Jesus has given us his body and blood to strengthen us for the journey ahead. Let us not always turn to international missions to bring Christ to others. We should start within our communities and be bearers of God's love to those we encounter.

Memorable Teachers Did you have a teacher whom you will always remember? A teacher who really went the extra mile to see that you learned something? I have been blessed with many teachers like that. The one who especially comes to mind right now is Truman Wiles, who taught me over thirty-five years ago. Truman had built a TV production studio at a nearby Protestant seminary when I was a seminarian. Back in those days, few people had ever had hands-on experience with TV studios, and we young folks were like bulls in a china shop. You might think that Truman, who had built this facility, would be very protective of it—that he would stand over our shoulders being sure we did everything just right. But, in fact, he let us experiment—even when we were not very delicate with these sensitive machines. I was impressed with his style of teaching—it was clear that his world was not about "me, the teacher" but about "you, the students." What can he do to help others grow in some new skills?

The Ascension Mission Just before his Ascension, Jesus gathers his remaining eleven apostles for one last time. For the past three years, the Lord has been their teacher. He has told them of the Father's love for them. He has shown them how to bring the healing power of God into a broken world. Now it is time for them to be the teachers. Jesus tells them to go forth and bring his mission to the whole world. Jesus asks them to hand on to others what he has given them. And then the Lord ascends back to the Father.

The first reading from the Acts of the Apostles also describes the Ascension. I love the last scene in that account. The eleven apostles are gazing up to heaven. They are just standing around looking. "Well, he's gone; how about that?" And they just look. Suddenly two men dressed in white appear. They say, "What are you doing standing around staring up to the heavens?" It is almost as if the apostles had not heard what Jesus had told them. He just finished saying they should be about spreading his good news. And here they stand looking up. The church is not for standing around; the church has a mission.

All Hallows Mission Some years ago, I was invited to teach at our Vincentian-run seminary in Ireland. This seminary was all about ordaining priests who would be missionaries. Nearly every new priest who came out of the seminary would be leaving Ireland to minister in other parts of the world. One afternoon while I was wandering around that wonderful old building, I came across a map of the world that showed all the places where their graduates were ministering. The map was centered in Ireland with all these colored strings emerging to the mission of Nigeria, and the mission of Kenya, and the mission of Costa Rica, and the mission of West Palm Beach, Florida. That caught my attention. But it was a reminder to me that our own American church was once a mission land. Years ago, believers realized that the church was not for standing around—the church had a mission. These folks would bring the faith to us.

Our Participation On this feast of the Ascension, Jesus calls you and me, as well as the first apostles, to be people with a mission. It is good that we gather here on Sunday for the Eucharist. It is good that we hear God's Word proclaimed and that we share the Lord's Body and Blood. But we do this not only to enjoy the Lord in our midst. We do this so that we are strengthened for the mission. Jesus calls us to spread his good news to others.

Examples of Our Mission This does not mean that we have to travel to Africa or other far-off places to be missionaries. Some people in our church are carrying the message to the foreign missions. We can participate in that missionary work by supporting them through our prayer and financial donations. We can also extend the charity of Christ far away by donating to those who will help the victims of the terrible earthquake in Indonesia. A good way to do that is to donate to Catholic Charities or to the Catholic Relief Services. There are lots of ways we can participate in the worldwide mission of the church.

The fact that we are to be missionaries also does not mean that all of us need to preach on the street corners of Valley Park. We can do a great deal of mission work right in our families, at work, or at school. Sometimes we might overlook those closest to us when we think of spreading the gospel. There may be people under our own roof who need someone to listen to them. Some years ago, Mother Theresa of Calcutta was talking to a group about her mission work among the poorest of the poor in India. At the end of her talk, someone in the audience asked, "I was so moved by your stories of your mission work. What can we do to help you?" Mother Theresa answered, "Love your children." The lady who asked the question said, "No, you don't quite understand. I am asking how we can help in spreading the gospel throughout the world." And Mother Theresa responded that she did understand. That loving your children as much as you can is the way God is calling you right now to spread the gospel. Spreading the gospel, being missionaries, very often means attending to those who are closest to us. And sometimes it means offering prayer and financial help to those who spread the faith to the far corners of the world.

Jesus as the Strength When Jesus sends these first apostles out to spread his Word, he does not say to them, "Get out there, gang, and do great things!" As if it was all up to their skills. No, the Lord tells them he will be with them. Jesus will be the power that makes their efforts bear fruit. He tells the new missionaries they can pick up poisonous snakes and not be harmed. They can drink deadly poison and not be harmed. I would not go near a snake, let alone pick one up. And if one ever bit me, I'd be off to the doctor right away. Does this mean I don't have faith? No, Jesus is not giving advice for us to go out and do stupid things. He is saying through these images that he will be with his missionaries. Despite the dangers and opposition they will face, he will be with them. He will be the one who gives power to their words and deeds. It is the Lord who is the strength of our own efforts to live the gospel.

Eucharist The Lord, of course, gives us his strength in this Eucharist that we celebrate each Sunday. Here we receive him who has given his life for us. The Eucharist is called a memorial, especially fitting on this Memorial Day weekend when we honor those men and women who gave their lives in military service. As we honor them, let us think of their sacrifice as an image of what Jesus himself has done in giving himself that we can have a full life. And in the spirit of the mission, let us ask the Lord to help us spread that Word to others.

Pentecost Sunday

Sacred Heart Parish, Valley Park, Missouri

June 4, 2006

- **Season:** The Holy Spirit, given to us in baptism, is the life of the church and life for the world.
- **Text:** The apostles lived in fear until the Holy Spirit entered their hearts and minds. They forgave sins and were empowered to continue Christ's work for the whole church. The Spirit may shock us at times, but through the gifts of the Spirit, we build up the Body, one person at a time.
- **Pastoral Context:** Ultimately, our gifts are from God, and we should be aware of how the Holy Spirit wants us to use our talents to be more present to others.

Having Spirit Sometimes, I rely on the internet to indicate how popular an expression is. Yesterday I entered the search term, "spirit" on Google and found about 450 million sites that used the word "spirit." The word is clearly entrenched in our language. It has a number of different meanings, but certainly of the important meanings is enthusiasm, as in we have school spirit. Those of you who have graduated or are about to graduate probably talk about that spirit. We know what separates lively people from dull, listless people. People who are alive are said to have *spirit*. So it is no accident that the Third Person of Blessed Trinity is called the Spirit. Not just a spirit of liveliness, but the Holy Spirit who is life itself.

Pentecost Scene Our scriptures on this feast of Pentecost give us various accounts of how the Holy Spirit is given to the church. Most telling is a line from the gospel that goes almost unnoticed. The gospel begins with the statement that the disciples were gathered behind locked doors for *fear* of the Jews. The disciples were afraid because the Jewish leaders were persecuting these new believers in Jesus. And they were *very* afraid. We know what it is like to be afraid—fear can paralyze us, it can keep us from taking risks. And fear did that to the little band of Jesus's followers—until the Lord stood in their midst and breathed the Holy Spirit on them. That changed everything. The Lord empowers them to set aside fear and even forgive sins in his name. We hear in our other readings how the disciples, strengthened by the Holy Spirit made bold proclamations of their faith. Their preaching could be understood by many foreigners in their own languages.

The Spirit is given to us still. It is important that you and I do not look back on this first Pentecost as simply a historical event that happened way back then over in the Holy Land. The Lord continues breathing the Spirit into our church. When you and I were baptized, we were baptized in the name of the Father, and of the Son, and of the Holy Spirit. All of us who are confirmed have received the Holy Spirit in that great sacrament. We call our bodies the temples of the Holy Spirit, and that is what they are—the Spirit is continually given to the people of God in this church. At this time of the liturgical year, many are given the Holy Spirit in the Sacrament of Confirmation—and some, in the footsteps of the apostles, receive the Spirit of ordination as priest.

Spirit Embraces our Humanness Pentecost is a special day for me because I was ordained a priest on the Saturday before Pentecost thirty-two years ago. Technically, the ordination Mass is the priest's first Mass since we do concelebrate at that Mass, but Pentecost was the first time I presided at the Eucharist on my own. And I faced a special challenge of faith that day. Up until ordination, it was easy to come to Mass and participate in this great sacrament. I had no difficulty believing that God worked through the priest as simple bread and wine were changed into the Body and Blood of Christ. But suddenly, on that Pentecost thirty-two years ago, it was these hands that the Lord was using. I knew myself—with all my ordinariness and faults. I had to realize that God had chosen to embrace this ordinary person to do wonderful things. It is about the Lord, not about us.

Corinthians—Strength of the Spirit That is what the Lord does in each of our lives. You and I will probably not go around preaching in languages that all foreigners understand as the disciples did in these scriptures. We will probably not be doing great healings and miracles. But the Holy Spirit is still very much alive in our persons. The Spirit will do wonderful things in our ordinary day-to-day lives. The Letter to the Corinthians tells us that there are many gifts of the Spirit in all of us. Some have the gift of patience, or understanding, or the gift of charity. These different gifts must be used for one another because we who have received the Spirit are one Body, one people of God. Desmond Tutu, the Anglican archbishop from South Africa, speaks of *ubuntu.* This is a word that is difficult to translate into

English. But people who have *ubuntu* have that special quality that makes them caring and compassionate. Other people truly matter to them—they are not little islands unto themselves. A person with *ubuntu* is someone who knows, "My humanity is caught up, is inextricably bound up, in yours," as Archbishop Tutu puts it. Is this not what our scriptures tell us when they say that we are one body, one people? Once the Spirit is here, we can no longer say that the lives of others are no concern of mine. The Spirit within us makes us all people with *ubuntu*.

The Spirit brings surprises. The Spirit also has some surprises for us. There was nothing nice and neat about the first Pentecost. Our scriptures tell us that the Holy Spirit made a rather startling entrance. There was a loud noise of a driving wind out of the sky. It sounds kind of like a tornado, doesn't it? That is a scary sound. The driving wind filled the whole house. If that were not enough, these tongues of fire parted and came to rest on each of them. My goodness. The loud wind brings a big crowd running to see what was up. And they experience this astonishing miracle of everyone understanding the preaching in his or her own native language. Who could have expected all that?

Ordinary Gifts There are some folks who have extraordinary gifts of the Spirit—they may show the wounds of Christ in their hands or do wonderful physical healings. The rest of us may wonder, "What about us? Does God not love us since we don't have those gifts?" I like the way a friend of mine put it recently. He was going to preach at a very special liturgy in the new Los Angeles cathedral. The event would be attended by a huge throng and would be videotaped. He became very nervous. He called his wise old grandmother and told her about all this and how nervous he felt. She said, "You just get up there and preach. This is not about you, it is about the Lord." That incident helps me keep all these scriptures about the gifts of the Spirit in perspective. All that we are given and do as followers is not about us; it is about the Lord.

Eucharist The Spirit of God now comes to us in a most powerful way in this Eucharist. We have a prayer at every Mass called the *epiclesis*—the prayer that calls the Holy Spirit upon these gifts of bread and wine. Through me, his human instrument, the Lord will take our simple gifts of bread and wine and make them his body and blood. As we receive him, may we grow in our appreciation that we are temples of the Holy Spirit.

Sunday Feasts in Ordinary Time

ONE OF DAN'S TALENTS as a preacher and pastor was his ability to make the great mysteries of the church approachable and understandable for his parishioners. For example, the Solemnity of the Most Holy Trinity has a notorious reputation among preachers who fear the task of addressing the theology of the Trinity with parishioners. Dan, however, was able to enter into the scriptures as a practical theologian and help the faithful see that the mysteries are still present and alive with implications for day-to-day life. Our Christian faith is not a theologically static reality disconnected from the living experience of the church. As a pastor, prophet, and practical theologian, Dan helped the flock by clarifying the meaning of the scriptures and putting the word into action in the twenty-first century.

Solemnity of the Most Holy Trinity

Sacred Heart Parish, Valley Park, Missouri

June 10, 2006

- **Season:** As we enter this great feast filled with awe and mystery, take care not to lose sight of what is most important: our membership in God's family.
- **Text:** The first reading from Deuteronomy emphasizes the act of remembrance. Paul calls us to realize the power of our baptism and recognize our identity as children of God. In the gospel, Jesus brings these two teachings together by encountering his disciples after his death and calling his disciples to bring more people into God's family.
- **Pastoral Context:** In this celebration of the Trinity, we recall our mission as a worldwide church. Through our belief in God, let us help

form disciples that recognize their participation and call to be members of the eternal family.

Remembering Our Past I was on my annual retreat all last week—can you see the glow of holiness? I hope I am a bit holier. I mention the retreat because I spent more time with the Lord this past week. I also spent lots of time with some of my Vincentian brothers from other cities. Some of the priests were from rather far away, and I had not seen them in many years. At meals, we told lots of stories about the old days. We talked about things we did in the seminary years and years ago. From the older priests, I heard community stories that happened before I was born. Our stories are very important. Even though I never met some of the Vincentians who died long ago, I need to hear their stories because it helps me appreciate how our religious community came to be what it is now. That is true for all of our families also. We need to hear those stories of our parents, grandparents, aunts, and uncles. It helps us appreciate who we are. God's family is no different. As God's family, we have our stories of the past that help us appreciate who we are as a church now.

Deuteronomy's Call to Remember On this Trinity Sunday, when we honor our God who is Father, Son, and Holy Spirit, our scriptures tell us to remember our faith stories. God's Word calls us to remember who our God has been for us all throughout the ages and who the Lord is for us now. The first reading from the ancient book of Deuteronomy has Moses telling the people to never forget where they have come from. He tells them to fix in their heart these memories: God created the heavens above and the earth below, and God created his people; God personally spoke to our nation; God befriended our nation and delivered us from slavery in Egypt. "As you remember all these wonders, my people," says Moses, "fix in your heart that he is God and there is no other. Never forget who your God is and what he has done for you."

God's Children by Baptism In addition to this call to remember the great things God has done for his people throughout salvation history, the second reading from Romans calls us to remember something special that God continues to do for us in making us his children. We have been baptized in the name of the Father, and of the Son, and of the Holy Spirit. We have become children of God and heirs who are destined to join the Lord for eternal life. We have been brought into a very intimate and personal relationship with the Trinity. We are not just creatures created by God and then sent off to fend for ourselves. We have been brought into God's own family through our baptism.

Remembering the Daily Miracles God has done wonderful miracles in creating us and making us his children. There are also plenty of smaller, daily miracles that go on all around us if we take the time to notice. If we ever wonder what God has done for us lately, we only need to look around our world. During retreat, I took more walks outside than I usually do, and I took more time to notice how beautiful the trees and the sky were. We have a magnificent world given to us. Some of the wonders of creation are more subtle—even unnoticed. If you use a computer, I wonder if you have thought about the fact that the silicon chip that drives all those calculations and paints those images on the screen, that chip is made from grains of sand? The creative power that God has put into a grain of sand. And then, of course, there are all those people in our lives who show us God's goodness and concern for us. Perhaps you remember a special teacher in school who spent extra time working with you—not because it was their job, but because they wanted to see us become the best people we could be. I am in awe when I think of all the special people in my life who have supported me through the years. If we ever get tempted to think we have made ourselves what we are today, we are not looking at life very unrealistically. God works through all of these people to bring out our best.

God's Love in Fathers and Mothers One of the special ways that God communicates his love to us is through our fathers and mothers. Parents have the special role of cooperating with God in helping their children become the mature people the Lord calls us to be. Let's face it, once in a great while, there is someone who does not have a good experience with their father or mother—I hope that is not the case for any of us. But even those who may have grown up without a father or without a mother, or who have had a negative experience with parents, are usually clever enough to choose a father figure or mother figure. They are able to find another person—a man or woman to look up to, to give them what parents give. They might not realize what they are doing, but they are choosing a father or a mother. I was fortunate enough to have had a very good father and mother. I did not need to find others. One important memory of my father stands out. When I was about five years old, I began to notice that children can be expensive. I noticed that parents in my neighborhood who had one child or none had lots of money to spend. There were six children in our family. So I asked my dad if he knew about this relationship between children and wealth. I'll never forget what he said: "Your mother and I would rather have all of you kids than have an entire barrel of money." I liked that answer. That's how God our father feels about us too. Each of us is precious in God's eyes.

Gospel Call to Spread the News In reflecting on all the things the Lord has done for us and continues to do for us on this Trinity Sunday, it is hoped that we are led to tell others about God's marvelous deeds. That is what we hear about in today's gospel. The gospel shows us Jesus meeting with the disciples after he has risen from the dead. He is about to ascend to the Father. Did you hear that little comment in the gospel that the disciples *doubted* it was Jesus? But even with this doubt, Jesus approaches them and commissions them to make disciples of all people and nations. As you have received God's wonders, Jesus tells them, go spread this good news. And Jesus continues to command that of us. We are to support a worldwide church mission with our prayer, or volunteer work and financial support. We are also to spread this good news to those in our own families, at school and work, mostly by our example. We have this commission too.

Fix in Your Heart Trinity Sunday is a time to think in threes. As we honor three persons in one God, our three scriptures call us today to fix in our hearts these three lessons: 1) We are to fix in our hearts that the Lord is God in the heavens and the earth—there is no other. 2) We are to fix in our hearts that we have been made children of God and heirs of heaven in our baptism. 3) And we are called to make disciples of all nations by the way we evangelize through our lives.

Eucharist Listen carefully to the words in our Third Eucharistic Prayer that we will use at this Mass this morning. It calls us again to reflect on the marvelous things that the Lord does in our lives. And it calls us to give praise and thanks. Let's come to this table with praise and thanks firmly fixed in our hearts.

Solemnity of the Most Holy Body and Blood of Christ (Corpus Christi)

Father's Day

Sacred Heart Parish, Valley Park, Missouri

June 18, 2006, 10:15 AM

- **Season:** Our life as Catholics revolves around the Eucharist because it is the food for our spiritual journey and unites us as a community of believers around the great feast of Christ's body and blood.
- **Text:** In the first reading, we see the earliest roots of the Eucharistic celebration in Exodus. Jesus advances the Mosaic covenant by instituting and giving us his body and blood in the Eucharist. God continues in covenantal relationship with the chosen people from the Old Testament to the New Testament.
- **Pastoral Context:** Communion is not a private endeavor. It is a communal act that unites us around the table and keeps us close to our God-given bond. Let us never lose sight of the significance of the Eucharist in our lives.

Blood as Life Force Men and women who work in medicine know how crucial blood is for our health. But our scriptures speak of the blood of Christ; they have a different meaning of the word blood. For example, when I went for a routine blood test a while back, I didn't look at first when the nurse drew blood because I am a big chicken when it comes to stuff like that. But once I realized that this did not really hurt, I did watch. Everything was very scientific, sterile, and professional, of course. This blood would later go through all kinds of special processes and machines to see if I am healthy. That is what we do with blood in the twenty-first century. But back in biblical times, way before any modern notions of medical science, people looked at blood very differently. They considered it to be the life force of an animal or a person even before they had developed that science. Someone noted that the mother pelican, for example, if she ran out of food, would peck at her own breast to draw blood that she could feed to her chicks. She was giving her life force. And in many ancient churches, you will see pelicans in the stained glass windows as an image of Christ who has poured out his blood for us. Blood as a gift of oneself permeates the scriptures on this feast of Corpus Christi, the Feast of the Body and Blood of Christ. On this feast, we celebrate the gift of Christ in the Eucharist.

Exodus: Remembering the Covenant Our first reading from the ancient Book of Exodus tells us about the roots of this Eucharist where Jesus gives us his body and blood. The ritual probably sounds strange to us. Here is Moses sprinkling blood on the altar and on the people. But remember that to these ancient ancestors in the faith, the blood of animals was their life force. Unusual as it may seem to us, this was their way of expressing in ritual that they were a people who had a bond with the Lord. They called this bond the covenant. They knew it was the Lord who had gathered them as a group of nomads and formed them into one cohesive people with an identity. It was God who brought them out of slavery in Egypt. God split the Red Sea so that the people could escape their pursuers. And God continued to work wonders for his people. "We must thank God for all he had done in this covenant," the people say. "And so we will do this ritual as an expression of our desire to always be bonded to God. We will always do his will."

The Ritual Routine Eventually, the Jewish people would build a grand temple in Jerusalem. They would do this ritual over and over. But people are people. And after a while, these rituals probably became rather routine. In our own time, we sometimes hear people say, "I don't want to go to Mass; it is so boring." Well, some of our ancestors in the faith may have said the same thing. They most likely did say, "Temple is so boring." Anything we do over and over can become a routine. It is most important that we remember *why* we do the ritual. Our ancient ancestors needed to remember that their ritual was intended to keep them close to their God, who had done so much for them. We need to remember that our Eucharist is an expression of that covenant. We must never let our celebration of the Eucharist become boring.

Eucharist—New Covenant It is clear from this gospel that Jesus has taken this ancient covenant to a new level in giving us his body and blood in the Eucharist. When Jesus takes the cup of wine in his hands at the Last Supper, he says, "This is the blood of the new covenant; it will be shed for many." When we celebrate this Eucharist, we once again enter that covenant, that bond with the Lord. We once again say that we believe there is a strong bond between our Lord and us, his people. We profess our faith that Jesus has died and risen for us—because he loves us more deeply than we can imagine.

We must celebrate Eucharist. Because God is so generous in loving us, the church tells us that we are obliged to give praise and thanks to God at this Eucharist, at least on Sundays and holy days. There are two ways to express that obligation. I could say, "I have to go to Mass," as if it were a great burden. I would rather be somewhere else more interesting. Or we could say, "I have to go to Mass" because if I do not, I am not really living out the covenant. I need to be here in order to express who I am as a child of a God and as a member of this believing community. That is what it means to have a covenant obligation.

Karl Leisner But there are some for whom the obligation to participate at Mass would seem strange. They would say, "You mean, you don't long to be at Mass?" One person who would have said that is a priest that John Paul beatified just a few years ago. Beatification is the last step before being declared a saint. This person is Karl Leisner, the only person ever to be ordained in a Nazi concentration camp. Leisner had been an outspoken Catholic leader. He had been especially active in helping Catholic youth in Nazi Germany stay faithful to their church. Remember, this was the time of the Hitler youth movements. Eventually, this seminarian was imprisoned at Dachau. A French bishop managed to visit him and ordain him as a priest. Father Leisner was so feeble at this time that it was a week before he could say this first Mass for other Catholic prisoners. Tell him that we are obliged to go to Mass on Sundays and holidays. His story reminds us of the tremendous privilege we have to be at this table whenever we wish.

Connecting Eucharist with Life When you and I receive the Lord at this table today, it is important that we remember this is not a private devotion—it is not about Jesus and me. We celebrate this Eucharist as People of God. Recall that St. Paul writing to the Corinthians had to chastise them because, although they were doing the Eucharistic liturgy just fine, they were neglecting the needs of the hungry and the poor. This connection between the Eucharist and our daily lives is expressed well in a story I read recently about a woman who had just become a Eucharistic minister. She had completed her parish training, but she was terrified on the first Sunday she was to minister. "What if I do something wrong? What if I forget what to do? What if, heaven forbid, I drop the cup?" And on and on her anxious thoughts went. But after a few moments, she began to relax as she reflected on the great gift Christ is giving in this sacrament. Later that week, she went to her parish soup kitchen, where she frequently helped feed the poor in her city. As she was dishing out soup, she handed the cup to a poor homeless woman, and she made a profound connection. She felt the same way she had felt when she was ministering at communion. This service, too, is a way that God touches people. And she realized, "This too is being Eucharist for people." As we come to this table, let us ask the Lord to feed us so that we meet him throughout the week in one another.

Solemnity of the Most Sacred Heart of Jesus

(celebrated by Sacred Heart Parish on Sunday)

Sacred Heart Parish, Valley Park, Missouri

June 25, 2006

- **Season:** God's love is not just an abstract idea. God takes flesh in Christ, who has chosen to love us from the heart.
- **Text:** Jesus loved by risking everything for us and suffering death on the cross. We see God's deep compassion and commitment to his people in the first reading, even when they turn away from him.
- **Pastoral Context:** Love is a risky endeavor because we expose ourselves to others who may treat us well or poorly. Following Christ's example, we shift from an attitude of fear and cowardliness to one that desires the best for others.

The Locus of Emotions Suppose we were watching the Science Channel or were watching *Nova* on PBS, and the question came up, "Where do we locate someone's feelings, their emotions?" (Make a frisking motion.) And like all good scientists, we would have to conclude right here (point to head). The scientists would tell us that the neurons in our brains produce electronic synapses or whatever happens up here. My apologies to any scientists if I go wrong. But they would say that our brains are the center of who we are as persons. Ask a scientist, "What happens with the heart?" They will say that the heart is a pump. It moves blood around our bodies. That is good and true science. But ask a woman who has just lost her husband of fifty years, "Where do you feel that grief?" they will never point to their brains. Love, whether in loss or whether it is a great joy, is here in our hearts. That may be inaccurate science, but it certainly is our human experience. We feel love in our hearts.

Vulnerability of the Sacred Heart This Feast of the Sacred Heart calls to mind that we have a Lord who has chosen to love us from the heart—and that can be risky. Something that helps me appreciate the importance of this Feast of the Sacred Heart is the film, *The Wizard of Oz*. I think I have seen that film more than any other since I was about six years old the first time I saw it. It was probably about the tenth time or so that I saw the film when one scene really hit me in a fresh way. You probably know it well. Near the end of the film, the wizard gives out the gifts to the scarecrow, the cowardly lion, and the tin man. He gives the tin man a heart. When it is time for Dorothy to go back to Kansas and they are all saying goodbye, the tin man says to her, "At last, I know I really do have a heart, because I can feel it breaking." When we love someone from the heart, we become vulnerable. That is why some folks find it very hard to risk love; they do not want to get hurt.

Gospel: Jesus's Deep Love Jesus did risk loving us in a very profound way, and he did get hurt. In this gospel today, we heard the moving account of Jesus's death on the cross. That is how far his love went for us. Our most recent Catechism of the Catholic Church says that Jesus loved each of us with a human heart. The catechism goes on to say that the Sacred Heart of Jesus is pierced for our sins and is the chief symbol of how our Lord loves us. If we want an image of what God's love is like, we look to the Sacred Heart.

Hosea: An Unfaithful People The tremendous love God has for us has very deep roots in scripture. Sometimes we have the mistaken notion that the Old Testament is all about a God who speaks from burning bushes and thunder. It is only when Jesus enters that we begin to experience a loving God. But the ancient prophecy of Hosea that we heard in the first reading shows us a very tender and compassionate God. Seven hundred years before the birth of Jesus, the prophet Hosea spoke this message of God to his people. It was a rough time for the people of God. If we think that our present church is facing difficult times, Hosea's era was a whole new level. It was a time when God's people had become very unfaithful. Many were not just lax about their faith; they turned away from the true God and were worshiping Baal, the pagan god. The people turned from God, who offered true life and happiness, to a pagan god who they thought could bring them happiness. They turned their back on God. Sometimes that happens in families. Sometimes we read about children who grow up and resent their parents for one reason or another, and parents and children don't speak to one another for years and years. It is a sad thing. For Hosea, family breakdown is a good image of how the people have turned away from God. Hosea uses images of marriage and family in his prophecies.

Hosea: A God Who Will Not Leave Them In Old Testament tradition, we might expect God to be rather angry with His people who turned to the worship of the pagan god, Baal. We might expect some thunder and lightning—a bit of smiting. But look at this Word. God talks like a loving parent. Israel is my son. When the people were children, when they were young people, I taught them to walk the way a mother or father teaches a child to take their first steps. God speaks tenderly through the prophet about leading his children out of Egyptian slavery. Despite all my love for these people, they have turned against me, says God the parent. But I will not get angry with them. My heart is overwhelmed; my pity is stirred. I will pick them up and hold them to my cheek. My goodness, what a powerful expression of God's love for us.

Parental Love I may have told you this story before—as I get older, I get a bit forgetful. But it is a story that I think captures well what God is saying in these scriptures about his love being that of a parent. It was about a young girl who really wanted her father to buy her a new car for her high school graduation. She had her heart set on it, as a matter of fact. She knew her father and mother loved her very much, so even if she did not get the car, it would be OK, but she really wanted the car. On her graduation day, she received lots of gifts from her family and friends, of course. But from her father—she received a Bible. She thanked him sincerely, but she felt a bit let down. But life went on. She went off to college, all was going well, until a few months into the semester, she started to miss her home, she got overwhelmed with study, and she was getting a bit depressed. For some reason, she picked up that Bible and started to read it, hoping that it would offer a bit of peace. And God's Word was very refreshing. She read on and on. When she turned a page out, fell an envelope. The note inside from her father said that he knew she really wanted a new car as her graduation gift. But he knew that she needed something much more lasting. He had given her this Bible because he knew she would need a strong relationship with Christ to get her through life. And, by the way, the note went on, if she would turn to the last page of the Bible she would find another envelope with the key to a new car. I'm glad she got the car, but I suspect she appreciated her father's concern for her faith even more.

Our Parish Model The father knew what would really sustain his daughter in life. God's Word on this Feast of the Sacred Heart is telling us that his love is essential to sustain us. This parish has the Sacred Heart of Jesus as our patron. Folks ought to look to us to be people who are devoted to the Sacred Heart, people who know where real life is centered. As we come to this Eucharist, let us ask the Lord, the Sacred Heart, to help us grow a bit more today in appreciating the deep love he has for each of us.

Feast of the Transfiguration of the Lord

Sacred Heart Parish, Valley Park, Missouri

August 6, 2006, 7 AM

- **Season:** The Transfiguration encourages us to believe that Christ's promises are true. He is truly the Son of God who has come to save us.
- **Text:** Just like our first reading today, Mark's Gospel brings us to the mountain, where we witness a scene of great hope and joy. Jesus reveals the truth and prepares the apostles for the realities that are to come after his passion and resurrection.
- **Pastoral Context:** Christ invites us to join the apostles and participate in the beauty of eternal life with Him. Christ also invites us to be peacemakers who bring the gift of hope to our world today.

Transfiguration—Mountain Top Sometimes, in front of church after Mass, I hear very young folks talk with great excitement to their parents about something that they saw in church or something they will do later in the day. Mark's words in this gospel sound almost like those excited children seeing a great wonder for the first time. We can pick up some of that excitement at the start of the gospel because we know something special is about to happen. We know something special is going to happen because Jesus leads Peter, James, and John up a mountain. This is significant because, throughout salvation history, God usually gives his special revelations on a mountaintop. In our first reading today, God tells Abraham to sacrifice his son on a height, that is an elevated area—probably a mountain. When Yahweh gave the ten commandments to Moses, it was on Mount Sinai. We know that as Jesus takes his disciples up the mountain in this gospel, something special is about to happen. And something special does happen. We hear God's Word proclaim that Jesus is seen in all his magnificent glory.

Transfiguration—the Encouraging Glimpse of Glory This gospel scene is a word of great encouragement to the disciples. They needed some encouragement just then because just before this glorious Transfiguration, Jesus had predicted his own suffering and death. This must have been a cause for great confusion and discouragement to the disciples. In fact, we know that Peter tried to get Jesus to stop talking about all this suffering and death nonsense. Peter was either too afraid or too unbelieving to accept the Father's will that Jesus die on the cross. And he certainly must have been downcast when he heard Jesus say, "Anyone who wishes to be my follower must take up his cross and join me." You mean we have to suffer too, Lord? But this glorious scene on the mountain today gives hope and encouragement. Jesus shows the disciples and us a glimpse of proof that all he has been saying is true. Although he will suffer and die, he will rise in glory. Death and suffering will be defeated. But this gospel is not just about the glory that awaits Jesus in the kingdom.

The Kingdom—Remembering the Promise in Times of Trial The Transfiguration shows us that we too are called to join the Lord in the glory of eternal life. This is not news to any of us. Most of us have known since we were children that we are called to enter heaven after we die. But I wonder how often we reflect on that great destiny that lies before us. That great promise was especially important for Mark's community—the first people to hear this gospel. Mark was writing to people who were very new disciples of Jesus. Most of us were probably raised Catholic Christians, and we have 2,000 years of history to tell us that this church is here to stay. But these early believers might have had their doubts about their faith. Some of them were facing persecution because they believed in Jesus. This account of the Transfiguration was, for them, a great source of encouragement in those rougher times.

Present Times of Trial In our own time, we do not face persecution for our Christian faith, but we still need events like the Transfiguration to give us hope and encouragement. The internet and email have brought something of a new sense of urgency for hope. Usually, at least once a week, I receive an email from some friend who is undergoing a special challenge. I hear from friends or friends of friends who are dealing with drug or alcohol dependency, people who are unemployed, folks facing serious illnesses. All sending emails asking for prayer. It can get a bit discouraging to see all of that suffering just in my own corner of the world. And then there is the evening news on television that shows us so much suffering in the Middle

East and other areas of war. Those are important times to think about who the Lord is in our lives and the hope that he holds out for us.

The Transfiguration calls Peter to witness. This Transfiguration is not only about the ultimate hope of eternal life after we die. It is also about having a spirit of hope in the here and now. If we truly believe in eternal life, that belief will make all the difference in how we live here and now. Our second reading today from the Letter of Peter calls us to witness that message to others around us. Peter was one of the chosen three to stand on the mountain and see Jesus transfigured in all his glory. And even though Jesus told him and the others that day, "This is not the time to tell anyone what you have seen," Jesus said you can tell them about it after the Son has risen from the dead. Now is that time. Peter says here in that reading that he is an eyewitness. He will spend the rest of his days telling others with all his energy about the Lord he had seen. And that is the mission for you and me too. Others ought to be able to look at the way we live our daily lives and see that we have let the message of the Transfiguration take hold. We believe the Lord shows us what our lives are really to be about in the future, as well as here and now.

Hiroshima—August 6, 1945 When Jesus was transfigured, we heard that he shone as a brilliant light. On this day, August 6, the world recalls another very powerful light. In 1945 on this day, the brilliant and horrible flash of an atomic bomb shone in Hiroshima. Over 100,000 people died that day, and many more died later as a result of radiation. There is a peace memorial in Hiroshima dedicated to a young girl named Sadako. This girl contracted leukemia as a result of the bomb. But she believed that she could recover. She believed that if she folded a thousand little paper birds, cranes they were, she would recover. Sadako wrote that "I will write Peace on your wings, and you will fly all over the world." She managed to make eight hundred of them before dying, but her friends finished the project for her. To this day, at the Hiroshima peace memorial, young people and others leave little paper cranes as a visible sign of peace and hope. When our Holy Father, Pope John Paul II, reflected on that event, he wrote in 1981, "To remember Hiroshima is to commit oneself to peace." This feast of the Transfiguration calls believers to witness to the way our lives could be when we take Jesus's message seriously, whether we are praying for peace worldwide, in the streets of our own city, or in our own homes. The Lord offers hope for what our lives can be.

Eucharist The Eucharist we celebrate now is a promise of the kingdom. Jesus has told us very little about what eternal life is like, but he did speak of it often as a banquet. The banquet of his body and blood at this table is meant to join us with him in preparing for the eternal banquet. As we receive the Lord at this table, let us ask him to increase our faith in what lies ahead for us. And let us ask that this belief in the kingdom will help us know how we need to live our lives today.

Solemnity of Our Lord Jesus Christ, King of the Universe

Sacred Heart Parish, Valley Park, Missouri

November 26, 2006

- **Season:** This solemnity invites us to contemplate what it means to have a lasting encounter with Jesus.
- **Text:** Jesus is not a mere earthly king. His kingdom is the source of light, truth, and strength.
- **Pastoral Context:** All are welcome and invited to seek truth in Christ's kingdom. Once we find the truth, we need to share this in all dimensions of our life (politics, economy, etc.). We must be advocates of the truth for the poor and oppressed in our society.

The Jesus Bolt One of my former students told me about his earlier career in the Air Force as a helicopter maintenance person. When he was training for this job, his grisly old sergeant was pointing out the various parts of the helicopter engine to the wide-eyed rookie. "This here's the rotor, sonny, and here is the exhaust system," and on and on. Finally, the old man pointed to a small bolt at the base of the rotor (make spinning gesture). "And this here, sonny, is the Jesus bolt." The young man, of course, wanted to know how it got to be called the Jesus bolt. "Well," the old sergeant said, "If that bolt falls out, the pilot gonna' see Jesus real soon." So the question for us is, "Do you want to see Jesus real soon?" Isn't that a sneaky way to get into a homily? But the question really is the central message of these scriptures today on this feast of Christ the King. Do we really want to see Jesus? Do we know who Christ our king is, or have we chosen to bow before someone or something else where we have gone to find meaning in our lives?

Tired of Earthly Kingdoms Some people are uncomfortable with the notion of Christ as a king. Maybe they have had enough of earthly kings for a while. It does get wearisome to hear about the constant fights between the Shiites and Sunnis who battle for power in Iraq, Jews and Palestinians fighting for power in the Middle East, and all those nations fighting constantly in Africa. We have also had so many stories of political intrigue and political assassinations in the news. We can only take so much of people killing each other at the direction of their kings and rulers. So what about this feast where Christ is hailed as a king? Why would we call Christ a king?

What is our King? Clearly, Jesus is not making himself out to be a king in the sense of any of these earthly rulers we know. In fact, Jesus says that explicitly in today's gospel when he tells Pilate, "My kingdom is not of this world. You don't see my soldiers running into your palace trying to defend me, do you?" In John's Gospel, the term, not of *the world* has a very specific meaning. For John, *the world* means all those forces of darkness and futility that will never give life. Those who hope to find ultimate pleasure in having lots of money, for example, are people of this world. Those who seek to lord it over others and oppress them with political or military power are of this world. The kingdom of Jesus is not like that. Jesus says here, "You will know that you have found the kingdom when you have found the truth." The kingdom of Jesus is not about money or power, but about the truth.

The Man Who Converted to Jesus This wonderful thing about this kingdom is that even the most simple and humble people can find the truth. You don't need an advanced degree to find Christ the King as the truth and center of our lives. I heard recently about an atheist who went up to one of his coworkers, Charley, at the lumber yard where they both worked. This man had led a rather wild life but then had a major conversion. The atheist said, "Charley, I heard you became a Christian. You must know a lot about religion now. Can you tell me where Jesus was born?" Charley said, "No, I don't know where Jesus was born." "Well then," the atheist said, "Where did Jesus do most of his preaching?" "I don't know that either," Charley answered. The questions went on and on until the atheist said, "Well, for someone who says he knows Jesus, you sure don't know much about him," Then Charlie said, "It's true that I don't know much about Jesus. But I do know that six months ago I was hopelessly addicted to alcohol. I know that I had lost my job, and my wife took our children and left me. But after I turned my life entirely over to Jesus, I joined AA and stopped drinking, my wife returned to me, I have a new job, and my children adore me. Jesus has done all that in my life. That is a truth I know." And, of course, this man has experienced what Jesus is saying to Pilate about living in the kingdom of God. This is what it means to live in the light of truth. The kingdom Jesus has brought is not like the fleeting kingdoms of this earth.

Where are the great kings now? Some years ago, I was invited to teach for a few weeks at a seminary in Rome. I had the pleasure of being there on the day that the entire country of Italy lost electricity. I am not sure it ever happened before—I guess I'm just very lucky. My room was on the fifth floor of the seminary that stood atop a rather high hill, so there on the top floor, I could literally see the entire city at my feet. Here was Rome, once the center of civilization. The emperor Caesar once could make entire countries fall with his slightest gesture. But that morning, a few years ago, it was all in darkness. The power was out literally and figuratively. Who cares what the political leaders in Rome decree in our day and age? Earthly kingdoms and political powers come and go, but the kingdom of Jesus is lasting. Jesus is the lasting truth.

Be involved in this world. This does not mean that nothing in this earthly life matters. Maybe we've heard some people imply that real Catholic Christians should not get too involved in this life if we believe in the kingdom of God. If you are dirt poor or have a serious illness, or if someone in your family suddenly dies, well, it's bad, but a really holy person knows that it's all for the best and that one day all the good people will be rewarded in heaven. That kind of thinking could cause people to be too indifferent to the suffering in this life. In fact, Jesus and our church call us to be intimately involved in the economic and political structures of earthly kingdoms so that the kingdom of God can take hold here and now—or at least start to take hold. Our American bishops remind us that working for justice is essential for living the gospel.

How serious are we? This Feast of Christ the King calls us to ask how serious we are about living the truth that Jesus has come to bring? When too many of the poor in our country have to make a decision whether to spend their money on medicine instead of on heat and food, where is the kingdom? When tensions break out between countries and the solution is to go kill as many of them as possible, where is the kingdom? We Christians need to let our legislators know that there is a truth by which we live. And we have a vision to offer. We'll never create a utopian society here in this life. The poor we will always have with us; even Jesus had to admit that. Wars have always been with us. But are we doing all we can to be people who stand for the kingdom of Jesus? It is about the way we vote, the way we get involved in our local communities, our parish, and our family. The kingdom is not only far off in the future—Christ is king now of every aspect of our lives.

Our Father When we come here to celebrate Eucharist, we say the *Our Father* just before receiving the Body and Blood of Christ. We pray that line, "Thy kingdom come, thy will be done on earth as it is in heaven." We don't just pray for that great final day when Jesus will return in majesty to bring all of this life to fulfillment. We also pray that the kingdom take a good foothold here and now.

Bread of Life Discourse

In reviewing hundreds of Fr. Dan's homilies, no other topic fueled his preaching spirit like the Eucharist. The Eucharist, central to our Catholic faith, is the ultimate source of our strength and grace as believers. In nearly every homily, Dan ended his preaching by reminding us that the celebration of the Mass culminates in our union around the table. This wondrous sacrament calls us to receive the Lord as beloved sons and daughters united as a community.

Dan's emphasis on the role of community within communion is essential in understanding his Eucharistic theology. We cannot correctly enter the celebration of communion without genuinely loving our neighbors and shedding the obstacles that hold us back from authentic charity. We all are children of God at the altar, given a chance to grow in faithful love with the Father. Dan Harris welcomed his listeners to the great feast. Dan's deepest desire was to make all feel loved at the altar of great sacrifice.

17th Sunday of Ordinary Time, Year B

Sacred Heart Parish, Valley Park, Missouri

July 30, 2006

- **Season:** In the lectionary for Year B, we now turn to the Bread of Life Discourse in the Gospel of John for several Sundays of Ordinary Time.

- **Text:** In the Old Testament, Elisha's trust in God's providence not only feeds the poor with little food, but the food overflows with abundant leftovers. Elisha's faith points the way to Jesus, the source of our nourishment in today's gospel.

- **Pastoral Context:** Just as with the multiplication of loaves and fishes, God can multiply our actions in ways that don't always meet the eye. Are we willing to see how he is calling us to act generously and courageously in the daily course of our lives?

More than Meets the Eye She was just a little African American lady riding on a bus. She was told to give up her seat to a white passenger. That was nothing unusual for Montgomery, Alabama, in 1955. That was the law—minorities had to stand if a white person wanted to sit down on the bus. This was a scene repeated over and over. But there was much more here than meets the eye that particular day because this little lady was Rosa Parks. And when she refused to obey the unjust law, she played a major role in setting the civil rights movement in motion. Sometimes, seemingly ordinary events contain much more than first meets the eye. Our scriptures are filled with such events. And our gospel and first reading are prime examples.

Elisha and the Twenty Loaves—More than Meets the Eye Our first reading, for instance, simply says that somebody brought twenty barley loaves to the prophet Elisha and the prophet said, give them to the people to eat. So what is the big deal? Is this simply a nice story about dinner? Or is there far more here than meets the eye? In Old Testament times, barley bread was the food often eaten by the poor. So we know first of all that God is once again taking the side of the poor. But twenty loaves is obviously not enough food to feed the many people gathered here. Elisha, the man of God, ignores the fact that the servant says, "This food will never feed everyone." Elisha, the man of God, says, "Feed all the people." And, of course, by the power of God, the bread was multiplied, and there was enough for everyone to eat. In fact, there is more than enough for everyone to eat. The story is about how God feeds his people, especially his poor, with more than enough. It is not just about bread made from flour, but it is a story about God being the very bread, the source of life for his people. What God did in the prophet Elisha's day, God also does much later in Jesus's time.

Gospel Feeding—More than Meets the Eye The gospel, too, contains much more than meets the eye. The gospel writer gives us a hint that this is going to be just an ordinary event when he starts out by telling us Jesus went up a high mountain. Many times in scripture, when an important revelation is going to be given by God, it happens on a mountain. When God gave Moses the ten commandments, it was atop a mountain—the mountain is the place for revelations. So we know right away in this that there will be something important revealed.

The story also takes place in that section of John's Gospel where there are many signs. Jesus performs signs, and the believer is asked to look into the signs—to look deeper into who Jesus is. When Jesus changed water into wine at the marriage feast of Cana, it was much more than a clever way to get new wine. The believer was to look into the sign, to look more deeply into who Jesus really is. So we are on the top of a mountain where revelation takes place, and we are in the midst of signs where we are asked to open our eyes and see more than meets the eye.

Jesus, as Elisha did before him, took a few barley loaves of bread (food for the poor) and also a few fish and fed five thousand people. And like Elisha before him, there is more than enough food. In fact, there were twelve baskets of leftovers. There is more than meets the eye here. This is not just another good feeding story. For those with eyes to really see, this gospel proclaims that Jesus gives himself generously as our food. Jesus himself is the source of our lives.

Some misinterpret Jesus. But some folks missed the point. They saw only a wonderful miracle and concluded that this miracle worker should be made their king. But that was not the point of the miracle. The gospel tells us Jesus withdrew from this group who wanted to crown him. The real life that Jesus was offering would not be based on political power or worldly wealth. The real-life bread that Jesus was offering was the kingdom of God, his very life. And the people missed another important part of the story—the generosity of Jesus that calls us to be generous sharers of our own resources. Jesus was able to accomplish so much with so little. It is no coincidence that a little child in this gospel has five loaves of bread and two fish. In Jesus's time, practically nobody had less power and fewer legal rights than a little child. Little children were the property of their parents. Here is this nobody, really, offering a handful of food—just a small gift from a small person. But look what the Lord can make out of that generosity. The young boys' few loaves and fishes fed a crowd of 5,000. Jesus can also accomplish a great deal with what we can offer.

The New York Cab Driver I read about a New York cab driver and his wife whose generosity is something like a modern miracle of the loaves and fishes. The *New York Times* and later *People Magazine* published the story of Om Dutta Sharma and his wife Krishna, who moved to New York over thirty years ago from their native India. Mr. Sharma drove a cab, saved his money, and was finally able to purchase his own cab medallion. Now that he owned that medallion, a license really, he was no longer obliged to give half his fare money to a fleet owner. The couple felt that they should not hoard their money but rather share it with the Indian village they had left. They visited their home village and gave $3,000 to open the first school for girls in the village. $3,000 might not seem like a great deal of money, but it was a king's ransom in the poor Indian village. Back in New York, they continue to help fund the school and a medical clinic. They did all this while putting two sons through college. The Sharmas said, "When we die, this material world is not going with us. What will be with us are the good deeds we leave behind." As I say, that is the generous spirit of the loaves and fishes—the good that can be done with very little. Have you and I fully seen the more than meets the eye in this gospel?

Eucharist Jesus feeds us here at the Eucharist, as he fed the five thousand in today's gospel. But it is not just ordinary food we receive. At this table, Jesus gives us himself and asks that we allow him to be the source of our lives. In receiving the Lord here, may he give us faith to see more than meets the eye.

18th Sunday of Ordinary Time, Year B

Sacred Heart Parish, Valley Park, Missouri

August 2, 2009, 8:30 AM

- **Season:** As a community, we continue meditating on Jesus, the Bread of Life.
- **Text:** In Exodus, we recognize that the Jews' forty-year journey in the desert centered on their escaping death from the Egyptians to attain new life from the Father. As the Jews took strength from the manna in the desert, we take strength when Jesus spiritually invigorates us with his life-giving bread.
- **Context:** Jesus calls himself the Bread of Life, which means that he is the food that sustains us in life's challenges. God wants to sustain us, especially in our profound weakness and painful moments. The liturgy invites us to let him enter our emptiness and fill us with his goodness.

Car Trips and Whining Some of our family are getting together this week up near Chicago. If your family is anything like ours, you know we will start to tell the old stories—the ones we have heard over and over but still enjoy. One of my favorite stories in our family is about the time in the 1960s when some of us drove from our home in Illinois out to California. My dad's major concern was that we make good time. He would not like it if we kids wanted to stop and see something that would delay the trip. We did whine enough to get him to stop at Meteor Crater in Arizona—that famous site where a huge meteor hit the earth 50,000 years ago. To our shock, Dad sat in the car while the rest of us toured the crater. I suspect he was annoyed that we had made this stop and put him off his schedule, although he never admitted that. When we got back to the car and told him how great it was, he said, "It's just a hole in the ground." It is not just the kids who whine on a car trip. We kidded Dad about that for many years—eventually, I think he found it funny. Most of us know about whining on car trips. Do road trips teach us anything about our lives as a church? The Book of Exodus knew all about long trips as a metaphor for life's journey.

God's people wander in the desert as a people. The Book of Exodus told us about God's chosen people, the Jews, wandering in the desert on their forty-year journey. They had been delivered from Egyptian slavery and were heading for their promised land. But it is much more than a story about people wandering among the heat and the sand. This is a story of God's people on a life and death journey. And there is much for us to learn about this journey. We don't just hear about Moses wandering in the desert or about Aaron, his brother, and their family. This is not about individuals or even families. This is the story of God's whole people on their journey. These people quickly learned that if they were going to make it through this very difficult time, they were going to need to rely on one another. No one person could do this alone. Together, they could do it. We, as a church, are much the same. Our faith is not about "Jesus and me—everyone else is on their own." We need one another on our lifelong faith journey. This is our story too.

God's people face trials. In addition to needing one another, we share something else with these desert people. Like them, our life journey has its own trials and challenges. These Jewish people struggled with hunger and thirst, sand storms, blisteringly hot days and cold nights, and on and on. While those are not our trials, we, too, have plenty of challenges as a. church. There are disagreements about how things ought to be done.

I grew up in a church where just about everyone did things the same way. You could walk into any church in the world and easily follow the Mass. The seminary libraries of the 1950s could fit in a relatively small room because there were not many different opinions. Most courses had one book. But things have changed. Some folks find it confusing that there are so many different opinions among believers. But we might forget that we have a long history of tensions. There was a time when different people claimed to be the true pope. Our history tells us that not all popes, bishops, or priests were saints. Neither were some of the folks sitting in the pews. Somehow, God has managed to hold this little church together through all of our own storms. But we sometimes keep whining about our church.

The Temptation to Give Up—the Whining God's people, as we read in our scriptures today, faced so many trials and were tempted to give up at times. We hear them this morning grumbling and whining (really) against Moses and his brother Aaron. "Why did you bring us out here to starve in this stinking desert? We had lots to eat back in Egypt. We want to go back to the good old days." We sometimes hear that same kind of thing in our present church. "Look what Vatican II did to our church. We want to go back to the old days the way it used to be. It was easier when the church told us everything we were supposed to do. We don't like this church." If anyone thinks I'm grinding an old axe, just take a look on the internet. It is filled with sites from Catholic groups that want to go back to the old days. They don't like the journey that we are on now. But God calls us to keep our focus on the journey here and now and the journey ahead. It's too late to go back.

What is manna? God heard his people whining in the desert, and God sent manna for them to eat. What is manna? It was probably some kind of flaky substance like a wafer, and it had a sweet taste to it. Where did it get that strange name, manna? One scholarly source says that the term manna might come from the Hebrew question, *man hu*? *Man hu* translates as "What is it?" People picked this substance up and asked, "What is it?" That is the best question they could have asked. Because God was giving more than just edible bread in the manna, he was saying that he, the Lord, was the life of his people. To ask, "What is it?" is to ask, "Who is the Lord?"

God is in charge. With that question, "What is this substance," and the question that follows, "Who is the Lord," we finally get to the heart of the matter in this story of desert wandering. This is the story of how God is the source of life for us, his people. Obviously, they needed help; they could not even feed themselves. It was not Moses that gave the bread from heaven. It was God that gave the bread from heaven. It was not Moses that finally threw off their chains of slavery in Egypt; it was the hand of God that freed the people. It was not Moses that led the people through the desert; it was God who appeared as a cloud by day and a pillar of fire by night. The lesson here is that God is the Lord. Without the Lord, we are nothing. Apologies to Dr. Phil, Oprah, and the whole crowd, but that is the truth. If we look anywhere else for the ultimate meaning of life, we won't find it. The Lord is life.

Jesus, the Bread of Life This is what Jesus is saying so strongly in the gospel this morning. He says that he is the Bread of Life. All the people who ate the manna in years past are now dead. Those who feed on Jesus the bread of life receive the food for eternal life. We are not just called to think about the things that Jesus said; we are not called to just try to do the things that Jesus tells us to do. We are called to be in a relationship with Jesus. He asks that we know him personally. He asks that we receive him as our food. He is the food for our journey through life.

Meanwhile, the journey goes on. Meanwhile, the journey goes on. Although we are at our best as God's people when we come here to receive the new manna, we have to go home to our families and to work tomorrow. We have to earn money, pay taxes, maybe take care of a sick relative, or drive the kids to their game. We are busy with many things. Can we make all of those efforts holy by realizing that they can be parts of our journey? For those who know our lives have meaning in the Lord, all of those things can be very holy. And we don't have to keep whining, "Are we there yet?" Once the journey is over and we are with the Lord, we'll know. We won't need to ask.

19th Sunday of Ordinary Time, Year B

Sacred Heart Parish, Valley Park, Missouri

August 13, 2006

- **Season:** The Bread of Life Discourse invites us to be church.
- **Text:** Elijah suffers because he has stood up for his faith in God. God continued to bless and strengthen Elijah, even in the pain and suffering he experienced in life. Jesus continues the Father's work in the Old Testament by telling his followers that he is the eternal bread necessary for our earthly journey. Even today, Jesus's eternal food blesses us

in every dimension of our life, the beautiful and ugly portions of our personhood.

- **Pastoral Context:** When difficult circumstances come about in our lives, it is easy to lose sight of God in the darkness. We should not believe that God has left us. Instead, God is blessing us and working deep within us to help us face our life struggles with his help as the church.

Are we blessed by God? How do we know if we are blessed by God? Some people think they are blessed by God if they are making good money, if they have a good job, if their family life is going well. Are those signs that we are blessed by God? Dr. Martin Luther King, in his "Letter from a Birmingham Jail," tells the story of someone who *knew* that she was blessed by God. This woman did not feel blessed because everything was going just peachy in her life. It was something else. Dr. King wrote about this 72-year-old African American woman who walked great distances every day rather than ride on the segregated busses of Montgomery, Alabama, in those years of the boycott. All that walking put quite a strain on her 72-year-old body. But she insisted on supporting the bus boycott. When she was asked why she went to all this trouble to support the boycott, she responded, "My feets is tired, but my soul is at rest." This woman did not measure God's blessings by what was perfect in her life. In fact, she found God's blessings in the imperfect, in the struggle. She found peace in knowing she was doing the right thing.

Elijah's Context: Was he blessed? I mentioned this woman's experience of blessing and peace because of our first reading. The great prophet Elijah certainly had done God's will all his life. We would expect him to be blessed by God. However, in the section we heard this morning, we find him praying for death. Our selection in the lectionary brought us into the middle of the story. If we go back a bit in this book, we read that Elijah was suffering because, like the woman Dr. King wrote about, the prophet had taken a stand for justice. The king's wife Jezebel had brought her pagan religion to the Jewish people and tried to impose pagan ways on God's people. Elijah, the last surviving prophet, would not stand for it. He courageously defied these false pagan prophets. It's dangerous to offend the king's wife and the king. For that loyalty to God, he had to flee the country for his life. And we see him today begging God for death. Here was someone who did his best to live his faith, and he faced what looked like utter failure.

Elijah and we struggle to do God's will. So that brings us back to the question—what does it look like for us to be blessed by God? Is success in our lives a sign of God's blessing? If Elijah teaches us anything, we learn that God's blessings are more subtle than we might think. If we struggle to live good lives, it does not mean that everything will be perfect for us. This means that couples may sometimes find themselves struggling very hard to make their marriage work. Parents may face many trials in trying to raise children as good Catholics. People who have been very faithful to God may find themselves suddenly unemployed or facing a serious illness. When all those difficult things happen to us, does it mean that we are not blessed by God?

God was with Elijah. We find the answer by going back to the story of Elijah. Notice what happens after old Elijah lays down under the tree. He has prayed to God to let him die. An angel walks up to him and places a hearth cake and a jug of water at his head. Elijah gets up and eats and then lies down for another snooze. But the angel comes back and says, "Keep eating; you need strength for a long journey." And strengthened by that food, Elijah is able to walk forty days and forty nights to the mountain of God. He did not have an easy life, but was he blessed? Absolutely, because he was strengthened by food given from God.

Jesus as Food for The Journey In today's gospel, Jesus makes it clear that he blesses us by giving us himself as the food for our own life's journey. Like our first reading, this gospel also has an important context. Earlier in this gospel, Jesus had been arguing with some of the religious people of his day. They were missing the point of his teaching. Jesus reminded them that God in the past gave their Jewish ancestors manna from heaven—bread that would get them through their desert wandering (not forty days of travel, but forty years of travel). And now, Jesus says, there is a new bread. Jesus will give them himself as the bread for life's journey. This is a very central message for John, the author of today's gospel. John wants us to hear, more than anything else, that those who believe in Jesus will have eternal life. And Jesus names the bread that will give eternal life. It is his own body and blood. This caused great confusion and even drove some of the disciples away. But Jesus holds his ground. Those who eat his body and drink his blood will have eternal life.

If we have the Lord, we are blessed. So, how do we know that we are blessed? It will not be measured by how much money we have in the bank; it will not be about whether our house could be featured in *Better Homes and Gardens*; it will not even be measured by how well our family life is going. We are blessed by God when we eat his body and drink his blood. "Our feets may be tired, but our souls will be at rest."

Eucharist—Turns Outward to the Church This does not mean that receiving the Eucharist is just about Jesus and me. This body and blood of the Lord empower us to look beyond our own little world to the larger church. The church is called Catholic precisely because it is universal and worldwide. A few times a year, we have special collections and appeals for foreign missions because we are a worldwide church. We are asked to be mindful of the poor in other areas of this diocese because we are a worldwide church. The one bread and the one cup make us one people. Years ago, when I was growing up, the common practice was to return to our pews after communion and just be alone in our prayer. Sometimes the choir would sing, and we would listen. But often, we are asked to join in a communion song. It takes a little effort—we might prefer to be alone in quiet prayer, and quiet prayer is good. But joining the community in song is one way of saying in a very practical way that this Eucharist is not just about Jesus and me. This one bread and one cup make me part of one people.

God gave old Elijah food during his long journey. Today at this table, the Lord gives us his very self as food for our own life's journey. Let us come here in gratitude and ask that we will always remember that he calls us to walk along with his whole church.

20th Sunday of Ordinary Time, Year B

Sacred Heart Parish, Valley Park, Missouri

August 16, 2009, noon

- **Season:** Jesus is the bread of life who wants to eliminate our physical and spiritual hunger by giving us the fullness of life: his body and blood.
- **Text:** The theme of wisdom underlies the first reading and gospel. We see that wisdom is not a mere, abstract idea in our first reading. The Israelites saw wisdom as a treasure that should be prized by all who receive it. In the gospel, Jesus is directing the people to realize that the gift of his body and blood is the wisest gift to accept because it brings us to eternal life with Christ. Jesus wants to enter his followers' lives as long as they are willing to take and accept him.

- **Pastoral Context:** As we are fed, so we are asked to feed others.

Nazi Refusal of Blood I ran across an interesting story from World War II that sheds some light on our gospel today. During the war, the Red Cross made blood available to all who needed it, allied soldiers and enemy soldiers. Some of the medics in the European theater started an intriguing practice. If a Nazi officer needed blood, the medics would try to see that it was blood donated by a Jewish person. The medic would tell the Nazi officer, "The bad news is that without this blood, you will likely die. The good news is, we have found a donor who is willing to give you their blood—it is a Jewish donor." Some of these officers actually refused this gift of blood. They said that they would rather die than accept the blood of a hated Jew. But many had the good sense to accept the generous gift. They at least showed a little wisdom. They knew that their lives were more valuable than maintaining their ignorant prejudice.

Gospel Offer of Life The scriptures today tell us about making the wise choice to accept the gift of life. For the last several Sundays, our gospel selections from John have proclaimed the gift of the Eucharist. Jesus, in this gospel, is offering his people the gift of eternal life if they will accept his body and blood as their life-giving food. He is offering them himself. But some would not accept the gift. When Jesus says that they must eat his body and drink his blood, some object that this talk is nonsense. Perhaps they think Jesus is talking about cannibalism. But when Jesus says he is offering his flesh, he is inviting us to embrace his whole person into ourselves—to make the body and blood of Jesus flow in our veins. A wonderful gift is offered, but some do not have the wisdom to accept it.

Lady Wisdom spreads the banquet. Our first reading tells us also about the importance of making a wise choice to accept God's gifts. In biblical times, people valued wisdom as a great treasure—people wanted to be considered wise. And so we hear about Lady Wisdom, who opens her luxurious house to those who want wisdom. She spreads a great banquet with fine food and wine. Those who partake of her meal will be wise. They will know what truly matters in life. But people will not partake of this meal unless they hunger for wisdom.

Where is our hunger? God's Word today asks us, "What do we hunger for?" Some of the people in the gospel came to Jesus just hungering for physical bread. After all, this is a poor society. When Jesus multiplied the loaves and fishes and fed them, many probably thought, "Here is our meal ticket." But they set their sights too low—Jesus wanted to offer them so much more than food for their stomachs. How about us? What do we hunger for?

I am still a bit haunted by an interview given by Mother Theresa when she visited the United States many years ago. She had spent much of her time feeding and caring for the poorest of the poor in India. But when she came to the United States, she gently said, "This is a very poor country too." Some people were astonished at that statement. But she explained how *spiritually* poor people were in our country. And it is true. Even in this difficult economy, when many folks are in serious financial straits, we don't have folks dying in the streets as they were in Mother Theresa's India. And yet, too many of us have not allowed ourselves to be truly hungry for the Lord in our lives. Do we hunger for real wisdom—the kind of wisdom that comes from the Lord—the wisdom that leads us to live in the Lord's ways? Do we hunger for the wisdom of knowing that only when we receive the Lord in our lives, only then are we really living the way he intends for us to live?

We need less stuff. Our culture, whether we want to admit it or not, is highly consumer-driven. It has been a bit astonishing to learn in this recent recession how much our economy depends on consumerism. Even if employment rises (and we pray that it does), even if the market continues to rise, folks still need to buy lots of stuff to get us back where we were a few years ago. The Book of Wisdom would remind us that we need to remember where real wisdom is found—and it is not in what we own. Our gospel reminds us that real life is not found in what we own but is found when Jesus is invited fully into our lives. This is not to say that any serious believer ought to give away all our possessions—that is not the point at all. But we do need to ask, where is our real hunger? What do we need to be truly happy in life? Have we set our sights too low? The Lord is offering us so much more of what will make our lives full. The Lord is offering us himself.

Feeding Others Our scriptures talk about hunger today, so I think it is appropriate to say a little about how we might feed others once the Lord has fed us with himself. Although Jesus is offering much more than mere physical bread in today's gospel, he does give physical bread to the hungry. Jesus is concerned that the poor and the hungry are fed. The news about world hunger is bleak. More than a billion people in the world go hungry. Each day, about 16,000 children die due to hunger-related causes. And before we jump to the conclusion that these poor, hungry folks live far away from us in third-world countries, we know that millions of children in the

United States live in households where people have to skip meals or eat less to make ends meet. Perhaps that is more so now than ever. This all sounds a bit overwhelming to me, and the temptation is to say there is just nothing we can do about this awful situation. We have plenty to do to take care of our own families. But of course, the question is one of priorities. You and I, who are fed by Christ at this table, can't let others go without food. I went out to dinner with friends last night, and I am sure many hungry people have never even seen the kind of meals that we all had. I think it is OK for us to enjoy a good meal once in a while—but that ought to remind us all the more about our need to help the hungry. And we are not helpless. There are internet sites sponsored by Bread for the World where I got some of these statistics. We can also learn more from sites sponsored by Catholic Charities and the Catholic Relief Services.

Eucharist Whatever way we choose to respond to the hunger of others, Jesus invites us to look around us and see that we are not in this alone. The one bread and the one cup at this table make us one people. We come grateful that he feeds us here. We say "Amen" when his body and blood is offered. There is no real translation for the word "Amen." It just means, "Amen." But when we utter that non-translatable word, may our faith-filled Amen be our way of saying, "Lord, I believe and wish to make you my food. As you feed me at this table, help me see how I can feed others."

21st Sunday of Ordinary Time, Year B

Sacred Heart Parish, Valley Park, Missouri

August 27, 2006, 10:15 AM

- **Season:** Christ, the Bread of Life, is the source of our love to build relationships with one another, including marital relationships and friendships.
- **Text:** How are we interpreting God's challenge to spouses? Are we willing to accept Paul's challenge to love our partners as Christ loves us?
- **Pastoral Context:** God wants us to affirm the goodness and beauty of our spouses. When we recognize our partners' God-given gifts and talents, we witness God's goodness and love in His creation.

Disregard what you heard. If you are a fan of courtroom dramas on TV, or if you have done jury duty, you know the famous line. One of the attorneys uttered something they were not supposed to say. The judge responds to an objection from one of the other lawyers and declares, "The jury will disregard what it just heard." What? I am supposed to pretend I did not hear what I just heard? As Christians, we are often told to do exactly that when our second reading says, "Wives should be subordinate to their husbands." The former translation is even harder to hear—"Wives should be submissive to their husbands." That notion is so offensive to our modern ears that folks pretend it was not there. In fact, our lectionary, our book of readings, gives us the option of using a version of that second reading that leaves out those harsh words. I know about a group of committed Catholic women who asked that their group members approach the pastor and the liturgy teams of their parishes, asking that they always use the shorter form of the reading without the offensive words. That's cheating. Those words are there in the scriptures. They do sound very harsh to our modern ears, but we can't take the easy way out and pretend they are not there. But what does the Word of God mean when it says that wives are to be subordinate to their husbands? Let's take a look at that message.

Mom was submissive. I grew up in this kind of house where a wife was expected to be subordinate to her husband. It was an old-fashioned kind of family, but I am a pretty old person, don't forget that. My mom made it clear to the six of us children that dad was the boss, the big cheese. Mostly. My dad liked to eat certain very strange things like cow tongue and calf's brains. You may laugh, but he really did eat those things. I have no idea if anyone does anymore, but dad did. And this was the one time I saw my mom waver a bit on the old subordinate role. I saw these calf's brains sitting on the kitchen table one day and asked mom what it was. My mom, who always spoke of dad with great respect in front of us, had probably had a bad day. She blurted out, "That's some of the weird junk your father likes to eat!" My little ears were shocked because I had always known mom to be very respectful and submissive. She would always treat dad as the boss . . . as I say, mostly.

Text Does Not Justify Arrogance It is important to be clear about what this scripture is *not* saying. God's Word is not saying that wives, or any women for that matter, are second-class citizens that must let men walk all over them in the name of Jesus. I am sure that all too often, there have been some rather twisted men who have used this text from scripture to justify their heavy-handed behavior toward women and children. "I'm the boss—it says so in the Bible." No person of common sense could ever imagine that Paul is talking here about lording it over others. Paul was the one who adamantly preached that we are all one in Christ. But that still leaves us with the question, "What is this text about?"

The Household Code We need to remember that St. Paul was a product of his own world. The ancient Greek and Roman world did not afford many rights to women or children. They were certainly not given much dignity. Part of Paul's psyche is that "this is the way things are—this is our world." He could imagine no other way of doing things. Paul wanted to write this letter about how we are to live as God's people. It was important that this new group, these Christians, live their home lives in a way that does not cause scandal to the non-believers. And the world was watching the new Christians carefully. People of my age or older remember something like this from our own world. Back in the 1960s, when John Kennedy was running for president, lots of strange people came out of the woodwork spreading stories about what would happen if our country elected a Catholic president. If we elect a Catholic president, the pope will rule the United States. Earlier than that in our history, some people believed that we were collecting guns in the basements of Catholic churches so that we could take over the country. People were watching. It was important for our American church to let people know that we are part of this country. "We live as patriotic Americans just as you are." Paul did now want the people of his time to think that Christians lived differently than others—we know how things are. But—we Christians have something important to bring to the world in terms of human dignity for all of God's people—men, women, and children. People of all races. Rich and poor.

Husbands, love your wives. Here is where the household code, the world that Paul lived in, is stretched much further. Paul goes on to tell husbands how they need to love their wives, not treat them as the pagans do. In other places, Paul talks about how Christ has come to bring full dignity to all people, no matter who they are. In Christ, Paul tells us, there is neither male nor female, Jew nor Greek, slave nor free. All are one in Christ. Jesus the Lord has made us one people of God where each person has great dignity. Each person is a child of God who is loved by God. And since each of us is a precious child of God, each of us needs to love one another. This is particularly important in the Christian family. Husbands and wives need to love one another and their children as Christ has loved us, his church.

Love is work. Love is so easy to talk about but so difficult to live. Again, I return to what I learned growing up in my family. I could see that my parents did not have an ideal marriage like the ones I saw on television. Everything was not just one blissful moment to the next. They had conflicts and tensions. But they also had that deep-down love that kept them working at their commitment. I believe they knew that love was sometimes hard work and sometimes about lots of sacrifice. One of my favorite stories from dad concerns the decision about where he and mom would live when it was time to retire. Dad's job forced them to move a number of times. They had always lived in quiet little towns where not much happened. I think that suited dad just fine. And I think he wanted to retire to a sleepy place like that. When it was time for them to retire, he asked my mom where she would like to live. She blurted out, "How about Vegas?" Dad told me years later that his heart really sank at that moment. But he felt that she had made enough sacrifices through the years that he was going to do exactly what she wanted. Sometimes that is what love demands—putting my will aside for others. And that kind of love is work.

Eucharist Where do we get the power to work at this kind of love? Jesus tells us in today's gospel when he calls us to root our lives in him by receiving his body and blood. That shocked some people; that caused some to walk away from Jesus, as we hear in today's gospel. But our answer must be the same as the other disciples. When Jesus turned to them and said, "So how about you? Will you too leave now that you know what I ask of you?" Maybe the disciples were still not sure what Jesus meant by eating his body and blood, but they did at least know that this is real life. And they said, "Lord, we're staying here with you." May we say that as we come to this table today to receive his body and blood.

Mary, the Angels, and St. Vincent de Paul

F<small>R. D</small>AN'S PASTORAL PRESENCE in St. Louis was not limited to Sacred Heart or St. Catherine Laboure Parishes. To bring "a year of Vincentian preaching" to a close, we include homilies from a few other communities where Dan preached and served. In each setting, Dan demonstrated pastoral sensitivity as he preached to the needs and context of his listeners.

Dan's preaching impact was felt and beloved by those who had the opportunity to hear him share and enter into God's Word. As one of his former students at Aquinas Institute of Theology, Erin Hammond, shares, "One of Dan's most important lessons he left with his students was always to preach Christ crucified. We have the crux of our witness and preaching through this understanding." In the selections provided below, we hope that Dan's messages on the church's feast days and solemnities may share a resonance with readers that God's Word is alive and active. The church lost a great priest and preacher with Dan Harris's death. Still, Fr. Dan's impact continues to be felt by those who knew him personally and those who encountered God through his messages of hope and love.

Solemnity of the Immaculate Conception

Congregation of the Mission Lazarist Residence, St. Louis, Missouri

December 8, 2010

- **Season:** On this Advent patronal feast day of the Catholic Church in the United States, we celebrate God's intention for Mary to give birth to the savior.
- **Text:** Mary dares to question the message of an angel.

- **Pastoral Context:** Just as Mary had faith in God to say yes to something unknown, we can ask for Mary's intercession when we do not know where God is leading us, trusting that our lives, too, can make Christ present.

Mary's Humanity What did Mary look like? What do you see when you see her statue? She is obviously someone very holy, rapt in prayer. She appears very serene, happy, very much at peace. But most statues show us the Queen of Heaven, the Mother of the church. The one who is now with the Lord in Glory. Today's gospel, on the other hand, shows us a very different glimpse of this woman. We see here a very human Mary, one like us. She is a young Jewish girl living with her family, engaged to a workman named Joseph. She is very much like any young girl we may know her age, preparing for marriage. But one day, an extraordinary thing happens to her. An angel appears and tells her she is to have a child. We who are hearing this story 2,000 years later know the happy ending. So we might miss just how shocking this news of the angel was to the young girl. To be told she is to have a wondrous child, she who is now a virgin. How can this be? And just what does the angel mean by a wondrous child? What kind of child will this be? The Mary in this gospel is not the serene Mary of this statue.

Mary questions the angel. This Mary has some questions of the angel. I have probably told you that some years ago, a Protestant preacher by the name of Thomas Troeger wrote a poem describing this gospel. He did not have the long tradition of Marian devotions that we Catholics have. When he looked at this story, something unique hit him. And so his poem of the Annunciation began this way, "Oh Mary, you who have the courage to question the word of an angel!" The poet really caught the spirit of this gospel. Something very challenging was being asked of this young girl, and she wanted to know how and why? If our comfortable world were suddenly turned completely on its ear, if we were asked to make a radical life choice that was the opposite of what we had been planning, wouldn't we have some questions?

Mary, the New Eve, trusts grace. But Mary trusted the answer from the angel. She was told by the angel that this child would be conceived by the power of the Holy Spirit. That the mighty hand of God would do all this. This is the work of the Lord, and she should have no fear. And Mary said, "Yes, thy will be done." In that instant, she became the new Eve. The woman we heard about in our first reading, Eve, was the mother of us all. But in giving her "yes" to the angel, Mary became the new Eve; the Mother of the church. God's grace was strong enough to help her in her questions.

The Woman of Atlanta Some time ago, I heard a talk given by another very heroic woman. She was a Presbyterian preacher who told the story of her own conversion to God's grace. As I think of her story, I cannot help but see the parallels with Mary's story in this gospel. This Presbyterian woman told how she had struggled to be a good wife and a good mother. Unfortunately, she had grown up with demanding parents whom she felt she could never quite please no matter how hard she tried. This was part of her forty-year struggle with depression. She carried that illness into her own marriage where she struggled with all her might to do everything perfectly for her family while studying for the ministry at the same time. Unfortunately, she kept meeting failure after failure. There were difficulties in her marriage; there were problems with the children. And one day, she sat down to pray, and she told God, "I give up. I cannot do it anymore. I cannot be perfect. I don't even want to try. I quit." And that is when it happened. God was able to get into her life, and his grace was able to pick her up and make her stronger than ever. When she was able to get out of the way, God could be strong in her life.

Our Call to Present Christ to the World And this is where we enter the story. This feast is not just a time for you and me to look at Mary and say how wonderful it is that she has shown Christ to the world. Because, if we have really been entering the spirit of Advent, we realize that we, too, share Mary's mission to show the face of Christ to others—especially in the way we treat them. But it means that we trust God to work within us according to his own wisdom. It means that we need to live with a few unanswered questions.

Realism—Present Christ where we live. When I realize that the Lord is calling me to share Mary's mission of showing the face of Christ to people, it is tempting to say, "Don't give me one more thing to do before Christmas, Lord. I've got gifts to buy, Christmas cards to send out, and all kinds of other things to do between now and Christmas. I'll get serious about showing Christ to others once I get through the holidays." That's precisely what Advent is about—a time of active waiting in which we are busy making room for the Lord to come into our lives. And to help others see the Lord in our midst. At this table, may the Lord help us to join in Mary's spirit of great trust.

Memorial of the Immaculate Heart of the Blessed Virgin Mary

Sisters of Loretto, Nerinx Hall High School, St. Louis, Missouri

July 2, 2011

- **Season:** While we honor Mary for her faithfulness to God and holiness in following his plan, we cannot forget that she was also fully human. She did not struggle with sin because of her Immaculate Heart, but she had to deal with the burdens and challenges of human life.

- **Text:** After Mary and Joseph experience the great fear of losing their child, they encounter Jesus following his Father's will. Mary recognized Christ's fidelity to the Father. This recognition is what scripture means when it says, "Mary kept all these things in her heart."

- **Pastoral Context:** Just as Mary suffered from witnessing her son suffer crucifixion and death, we carry pains and miseries in our hearts. Rather than allow those pains to dictate how we live our lives, let us follow Mary's example and turn to God to seek his healing and consolation.

Remember that she was human. Mary has been depicted in some rather amazing and beautiful statues and stained glass. The church at our motherhouse in Perryville has a magnificent rendition of her assumption into heaven. I remember well looking at that art for a long time while praying in the chapel. With all of that magnificent art, it is sometimes difficult to remember that Mary was a human person, one of us. She experienced all of the normal aspects of life we do (of course, without sin). This Feast of the Immaculate Heart, at least the gospel for this feast, gives us an excellent opportunity to reflect on her very human side. A goddess would have understood when Jesus said I must be about my Father's business in my Father's house. Mary, a human, did not understand.

Ignatian Prayer In a spirit of Ignatian prayer, I imagined myself in the Jerusalem temple right at the moment that Mary and Joseph encountered Jesus talking with the wise teachers. This is their child who has been missing from the caravan. You and I have seen mothers on the evening news begging for the return of their lost children. For a mother to lose a child. And I stood in the temple, I tried to see Mary's reaction when this child said in effect, "I am not sure why you came back looking for me; I am doing what I am supposed to be doing."

Love involves sorrow. The last line of today's gospel gives us a scriptural basis for this feast. God's Word simply says, "And Mary kept all these things in her heart." Ever kept something in your heart? Of course. All that truly matters, all those we really care about, are kept always in our hearts. And that is not always a pleasant experience. Sometimes, as we well know, the things we must carry in our heart have an edge of sadness to them. I carry some folks in my heart every day who have died. I'll bet you do too. It is part of being human; it is an experience that Mary has shared with us.

Eucharist As we honor the great compassion of the Mother of God in this feast, let us ask her to join us at this table where, with Jesus, we offer praise and thanks to the Father.

Solemnity of the Assumption of the Blessed Virgin Mary

Sisters of Loretto, Nerinx Hall High School, St. Louis, Missouri

August 15, 2009

- **Season:** Mary's Assumption represents a call to faithful devotion to God and a witness that God's goodness will triumph over evil.
- **Text:** In the first reading, we learn about the persecution of the early Christians under Roman authorities. While people questioned whether it was worthwhile to stay Christian and follow God, Revelation reveals that God is with those members who are struggling and suffering to follow him. In the gospel, Mary's Magnificat expresses God's fidelity to creation. God will always protect, strengthen and guide the church away from evil and toward true goodness and beauty.
- **Pastoral Context:** Mary's Assumption serves as a reminder that God is always with us. When his plans seem most confusing or difficult, he is there to bolster us and give us the hope to find our life's true purpose.

It's not the old church. You and I are not living in the same church we grew up in. Sure, this is still the church founded by Christ, this is still the Mystical Body, but things are very different on the level of how we interact as a church. That has led many folks to leave us. When I read stories about the giant megachurches with their carefully choreographed music and the fancy television effects, invariably, someone who is interviewed in the congregation says, "I used to be a Catholic, but this church is much more to my liking." When I think about the dwindling number of priests and religious sisters, I sometimes wonder what the future of our church will be—at least in the United States and in some parts of the world. These are very real and important issues. But it is important for us to realize that this is not the first time in history that the church has had to deal with serious problems. As our first reading today from the Book of Revelation shows us, we have faced tough issues from the day we first became a church.

Revelation—The early church faces persecution. The infant church was under a severe persecution from the Roman civil authorities. Christians were being tortured and put to death for their faith. They must have wondered, "Did we make the right decision becoming a Christian? Why does everyone around us criticize us for our beliefs? Is there any future to this church? Will it survive?" Although our own church today is not under physical persecution, those old questions from our ancestors in the faith are being asked by many people in our own time. Is there a future to this church?

Revelation—The Promise of Triumph, Then and Now The reading from the Book of Revelation answers those difficult questions with a resounding "Yes—the Lord is with this struggling church." The human authors of this inspired book used coded language to talk about the early church. The book speaks of dragons, a woman standing with the moon at her feet, and other wonders. But the ancient believers, the original audience, knew what it all meant. The woman is a symbolic way to describe the church under persecution. She is pursued by the dragon that stands for those evil forces trying to destroy the church. The good news in the reading is that the woman is protected from the evil dragon. She triumphs over the evil forces. The early believers heard this as very good news indeed. It was God's Word telling them to keep up the good fight, to be faithful; the church will survive and triumph over its persecutors. And indeed it did. But this is more than a history lesson for us living today. This word continues to tell us that we have made the right choice in following the Lord. We, too, are assured that God's strength is with us to help us triumph over difficulty.

Feast of Assumption—Applies "Woman" to Mary On this feast of the Assumption of Mary into heaven, the church has taken this reading and applied it to Mary. Even though the sacred author originally intended this woman to stand for the church under persecution, the woman here has come to symbolize Mary, who is a visible proof to us that all of this promise is true. We heard, for example, in our second reading today that because Jesus Christ has risen from the dead, we too will someday rise from the dead. A wonderful promise, but how do we know anyone besides Jesus will rise from the dead? That's partly what this Feast of the Assumption is about. Mary, the Mother of God, is assumed bodily into heaven. She is proof. Mary's Assumption is a strong testimony that the eventual triumph over evil promised in God's Word is a reality. That is enough to encourage anyone to be faithful to the life we are called to. But we don't have to wait until we get to heaven for the triumph to begin. Mary's life is a strong testimony that the triumph begins here and now in our everyday lives.

The Magnificat—God is at work now! In the gospel, we get a glimpse of Mary rejoicing in the fact that the triumph starts here and now. She is aware that God has begun a wonderful work inside her as Jesus begins to grow in her womb. In her enthusiasm, she goes to visit Elizabeth, and she utters this marvelous prayer, *The Magnificat*. "My being proclaims the greatness of the Lord. . . . He has shown might with his arm. . . . He has deposed the mighty from their thrones and raised the lowly to high places." This Magnificat re-echoes the language of the Book of Revelation that tells us God is stronger than any force that would attack his people, the church; in God, the church will triumph. Mary is so excited and enthusiastic here as she reflects on the wonderful things God does in our lives. It would be good for you and me, who say this prayer every day, to think about how "my" being, yours and mine, proclaims the greatness of the Lord. The prayer says that when God is at work in us, anything can happen. People can truly change. Old dogs can learn new tricks.

Nobel's Conversion My favorite story about someone starting over with a fresh outlook on life involved a man who lived about ninety years ago. He picked up the newspaper one morning, and to his horror, he found his own obituary. By mistake, someone reported that he had died. After he got over the shock of seeing the obituary, he decided to read it to find out what people had said about him. He had been a successful inventor who, among other things, invented dynamite. The products of his company were used extensively in warfare. The obituary said, "Merchant of Death dies." That bothered him. He did not want to be remembered as a merchant of death. And so Alfred Nobel began awarding the Nobel Peace Prize. And that is now what he is most known for—not as a merchant of death, but a promoter of peace. Old dogs can learn new tricks. People can rediscover what their lives are supposed to be about. Who knows what wonders can God work in our lives?

God's Word and this feast offer hope. This Feast of the Assumption is about surprises and wonders that God can work in our lives and does work in our lives. Not only does the Lord call us to begin again with enthusiasm in our faith, but the Lord also promises us that he is with us on our journey. The Lord was with the people who needed this vision of the dragon and the woman in the Book of Revelation. The Lord was with Mary as she uttered the hopeful prayer, the Magnificat, and the Lord is with us as we live our faith day in and day out in this church. This is especially important for us to realize at times when it is difficult to live our faith in a skeptical world. In this Eucharist, let us ask the Lord to fill us with the same spirit that he gave to Mary so that we can make her prayer our prayer. Let us be able to also say, "My being proclaims the greatness of the Lord."

Feast of Archangels Michael, Gabriel, and Raphael

Aquinas Institute of Theology, St. Louis, Missouri

September 29, 2005

- **Season:** Just as the archangels bring God's presence into the world, we, too, are meant to authentically communicate God's presence to those around us,

- **Text:** Jesus recognizes Nathanael's authentic witness to the faith. After Christ has recognized him as a devout and faithful man, Nathanael can identify Jesus as the true Son of God.

- **Pastoral Context:** The church calls those of us who have been transformed in a living encounter with Jesus to bear authentic witness of this faith to others.

The Real Thing Jesus and I have a great deal in common. (If they laugh—I'm crushed that you have not noticed.) One thing I do have in common with Jesus, and I believe you do too, is the ability to spot a true follower of the Lord—a real disciple. When Jesus saw Nathanael, he pronounced him to be a true Israelite. The Greek word is *alethos*. Nathanael is an *alethos* Israelite, not in the sense that this person is really an Israelite, but *alethos* in the sense that this person is the real thing. This is a true believer. As this Gospel of John begins, Nathanael is not one of the skeptics who has come to scoff at the preaching of Jesus. Nathanael is the real thing.

Cosgrove Retirement Before I joined the Aquinas faculty last year, I ministered at a seminary in California for eight years. Most of those years, I went to a nearby parish each Sunday to celebrate Eucharist. The pastor was a delightful man, Joe Cosgrove, whom I had really come to respect. When he retired this past summer, I went back for his party. I don't like to travel, and as a card-carrying introvert, I don't like crowded social gatherings. But I would not have missed this retirement party. The hotel ballroom was jammed with parishioners at the dinner because everyone wanted to be there. In my brief talk, I told the group I flew across the country for this dinner to spend a few hours honoring a minister who is the real thing. Joe, the pastor, is *alethos,* as is Nathanael. How refreshing it is to see the real thing—a man or woman who shows us the face of God.

Nathanael sees the real thing. After Jesus points out that Nathanael is the real thing, a true believer, Nathanael returns the compliment by announcing that Jesus is the real thing. Nathanael says, "I can see that you are the Son of God; you are the king of Israel." We can be sure that this new disciple spent the rest of his life telling others about the Lord he had met. Nathanael gives us, in that brief confession of faith, a succinct model of who we are to be as ministers. We are called to tell others about the Lord we have come to know. Paul VI talked about this aspect of ministry in his brief but haunting observation that modern men and women no longer listen to teachers. They will listen to a witness. If people do listen to teachers, Paul VI said, it is only because they are also witnesses. You and I are called to be ministers who have met the Lord and are now on fire to let others know whom we have come to know and love. For his good eye in spotting the Lord, Jesus says that Nathanael will see greater things—Jesus recalls the Genesis passage where Jacob saw God's messengers, the angels on the ladder between heaven and earth.

Angels Today, we honor the three archangels, Michael, Gabriel, and Raphael, who also show us the face of God. In today's Liturgy of the Hours, Gregory the Great reminds us that the word *angel* is not so much about a nature but about a function. Angels, especially the archangels Michael, Gabriel, and Raphael, describe specific ways that the Lord is active in our lives. The name Michael means "Who Is Like God?" Michael is the powerful arm of the Lord—far more powerful than the evil that threatens true believers. Gabriel, "The Strength of God," was sent to Mary to announce a

God strong enough to truly embrace our human nature while remaining God. And Mary was strong enough to ask an angel, "How can this be?" Raphael means "God's Remedy." Raphael touched the eyes of Tobit and brought God's healing to him. Clearly, the Lord is active in our lives as expressed in this feast of the angels.

Vincent A few days ago, on the feast of St. Vincent de Paul, the founder of my community, Dominic Holtz gave us an eloquent description of Vincent. Dominic was kind enough to leave out the part we might call Vincentgate. Vincent was not a model priest early in his career. He was interested in an easy, comfortable life and a good income. But then Vincent, like St. Paul, like Nathanael, met the Lord, and he was never the same again. That encounter with the Lord changes people forever. And those who have met the Lord can never stop introducing others to the Lord they have met. Let us come now to this table to meet this Lord who is the real thing.

Solemnity of St. Vincent de Paul

Congregation of the Mission Lazarist Residence, St. Louis, Missouri

September 27, 2010

- **Season:** St. Vincent de Paul was inspired by the gospel to seek out those who have been excluded in society and bring them to God. He saw beauty in God's little ones and wanted others to recognize their goodness as children of God.

- **Text:** The *anawim* of God includes those on the margins or peripheries of society who need God's help. God loves them deeply.

- **Pastoral Context:** When we reflect on whether we are living out the beatitudes, it may be worthwhile to consider how often we allow God to guide our thoughts and actions in relation to God's little ones.

Russ was one of the little ones. Years ago, there was a wonderful old man named Russ who used to take care of the faculty automobiles at Kenrick Seminary. Russ loved to tell stories. In fact, if he caught your ear, you could end up listening to him for quite a while. One day Hugh O'Donnell, who was the rector of the seminary, came running past me saying that he was almost late for an appointment with the cardinal. I happened to look out my window and saw that he had run into Russ at the garage. And there they stood talking. Later that day, I asked Hugh if he had been late for his meeting. He told me that yes, he arrived late, and yes, the cardinal was not pleased about him being late. But he told me, "If you don't have time for people like Russ, you don't understand what it means to be a Christian." I thought about that for a long time. Although Russ was not important in the ways that most people judge importance, he was one of God's little ones. And we need time for them.

God's Little Ones Russ was the kind of person that our gospel is talking about today—God's little ones. And he is the kind of person that Vincent de Paul would have noticed. The scriptures use the term *anawim* to describe the little ones of God. The *anawim* are not the movers and shakers of society. They are often the poor, the widows and orphans, the powerless. And precisely because they are powerless and so easily taken advantage of, God shows them a special concern. God always has cared especially for his *anawim*.

Beatitudes: Signs of a New Life The little ones trust because they have the Lord for their treasure. In the beatitudes in today's gospel, Jesus gives us an image of what it looks like in a person when the Lord is our treasure. I heard a preacher once refer unfortunately to the beatitudes as "helpful hints to happiness." It was an unfortunate characterization because it implies all we have to do is go out there and be poor in spirit, be meek, and be happy when we are persecuted for our faith. We can't accomplish that by ourselves. This is not really in our human power. This kind of life is the work of the Lord in our lives. Jesus is not telling us to pull ourselves up by our spiritual bootstraps and act this way. He is saying that when *his* life is in us, this is how we will want to live. Those who treasure the Lord do not treasure personal wealth, prestige, or privilege. They are the little ones who really "get it."

The Test How do we know if we are people of the Beatitudes—if the Lord is really our treasure? One way to know is to honestly ask ourselves how our lives reflect what we value. Specifically, I can ask myself, "How do I spend my time, my energy, and my money?" That is a challenging test. And when I do look at how I spend my time, my energy, and my money, I see that I have a lot of growing to do. The Lord is not my treasure fully yet, but I hope I am on the way. And I believe we are all on the way.

Eucharist In this Eucharist today, we are fed with the Lord's body and blood. The little ones in this world usually rely on others to feed them. As the Lord feeds us, let us ask to be little enough to have him as the center of our lives.

CPSIA information can be obtained
at www.ICGtesting.com
Printed in the USA
BVHW032135191122
652312BV00002B/5